ONTHEREDBOX

The Power of the Gospel
Rediscover The Message of the Cross

Copyright © 2020 by Jacob Bock

Published by: **Ontheredbox**
Puerta del Sol 4, 5ª Planta
28013 Madrid, Spain
http://www.ontheredbox.com/en
facebook.com/ontheredbox

All rights reserved. No part of this publication may be reproduced, stored in a retrieval system, or transmitted in any form by any means, electronic, mechanical, photocopy, recording, or otherwise including all subsidiary use and use in electronic and digital formats not yet created without the prior permission of the publisher, except as provided for by USA and international copyright law.

First Printing 2020

Unless otherwise indicated, Scripture references are from The Holy Bible: ESV English Standard Version®. Copyright © 1973, 1978, 1984 by International Bible Society. Used by permission of Zondervan Publishing House. All rights reserved.

The "ESV" and "English Standard Version" trademarks are registered in the United States Patent and Trademark Office by International Bible Society. Use of either trademark requires the permission of International Bible Society.

THE POWER *of* THE GOSPEL

REDISCOVER THE MESSAGE OF THE CROSS

By
JACOB BOCK

CONTENTS

INTRODUCTION   11

CHAPTER ONE
THE PROBLEM • 13

Column One: The Law   15
The Law Reveals You Are a Sinner   19
The Law Reveals You Are Guilty   21
The Law Reveals You Are Dead   23
The Law Reveals You Are a Slave   25
The Law Reveals You Are Dirty   27
The Law Reveals You Are an Enemy of God   29
The Law Reveals You Are Under His Wrath   33
Review   34
Final Remarks   34

CHAPTER TWO
THE CONSEQUENCE • 39

Column Two: Eternity   41
1. Death   42
2. Judgement   45
3. Hell   49
4. Heaven   53
5. Review   53
6. Final Remarks   54

CHAPTER THREE
THE SOLUTION • 57

Column Three: The Cross of Christ   60
Forgiven - Jesus Takes Your Place   63
Innocent - Jesus Justifies You   67
Alive - Jesus Regenerates You   71
Free - Jesus Redeems You   75
Clean - Jesus Sanctifies You   79
Friend - Jesus Reconciles You   83
Loved - Jesus Is Your Propitiation   87
The Resurrection   90
Review   91
Final Remarks   92

CHAPTER FOUR
OUR RESPONSE • 93

Column Four: Repentance and Faith   97
Crossing the Cross   97
What Is Repentance?   98
The Power of the Holy Spirit   98
How Do I Repent?   98
What Is Faith?   100
Review   102
Final Remarks   103

REVIEW OF THE FOUR COLUMNS   105

CONCLUSION   107

Written for all Christians who have a desire to better understand the gospel message and to learn to communicate it with power

Special thanks to:

Julie Bock

Scott Harrup
Paul Collins
Olivier Darbonville

(Did you really think I could write this book by myself?)

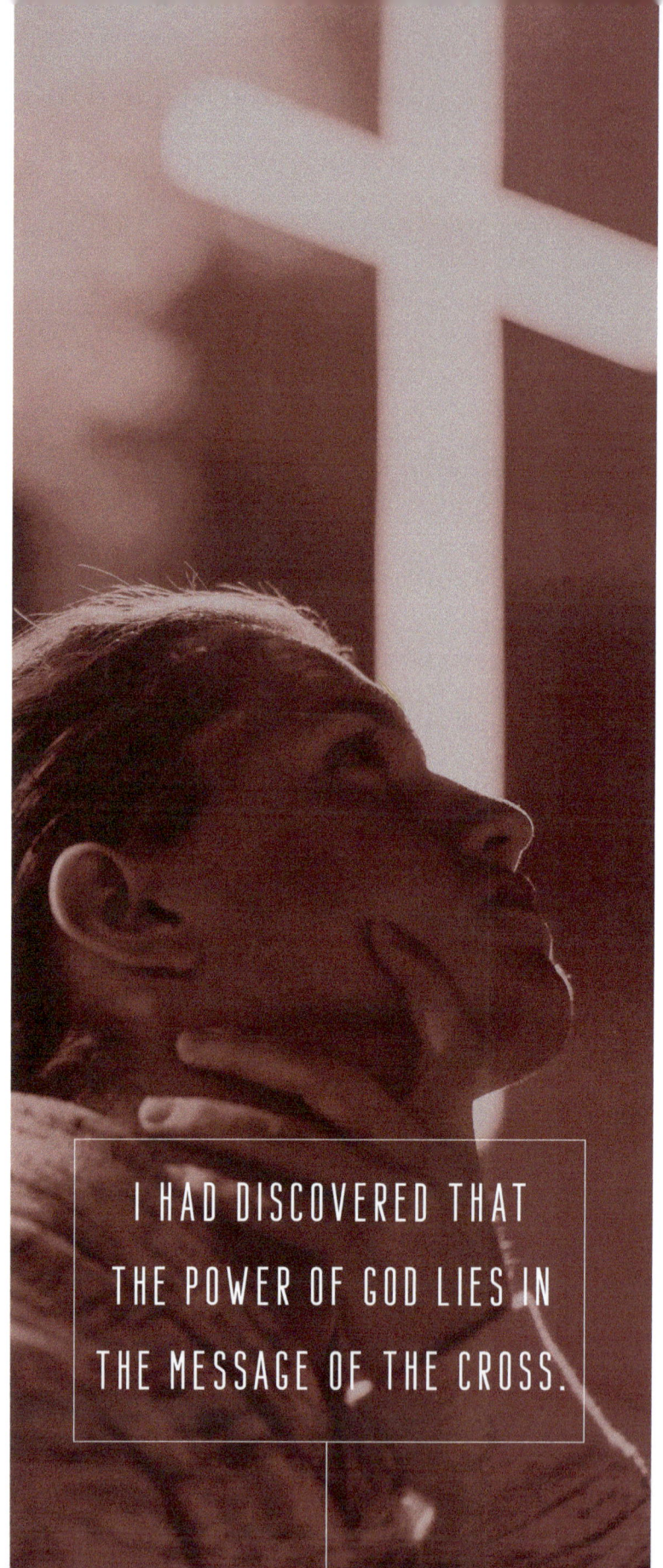

I had no idea what was about to hit me. I had been a follower of Jesus for 18 years and a missionary in Spain for ten of those years. I had experienced the power of the gospel and the Holy Spirit in a number of ways, but nothing like what I was about to experience.

In October 1997, I attended an evangelistic service in America. There was an amazing outpouring of the Holy Spirit in a church, and I wanted to be a part of it.[1] I walked in on a Wednesday night and took a seat. Steve Hill, the evangelist, took his place behind the pulpit and opened his Bible to Romans chapter two and began to read:

> "Or do you presume on the riches of his kindness and forbearance and patience, not knowing that God's kindness is meant to lead you to repentance? But because of your hard and impenitent heart, you are storing up wrath for yourself on the day of wrath when God's righteous judgement will be revealed."[2]

He then explained how the more we sinned, the more the wrath of God was building up like water behind a dam. On Judgement Day, the dam would break and the wrath of God would sweep us away!

---

[1] The Brownsville revival in Pensacola Florida lasted from 1996 until 2001.
[2] Romans 2:4,5

I vividly remember feeling such an intense conviction of the Holy Spirit in my heart. He was pointing out a host of sins I still had lodged there. My heart raced, and the fear of God overwhelmed me. I began to loathe my sin. I had the urge to run to the altar and repent, but I couldn't because Steve had just begun to preach.

Then he began to proclaim the kindness and patience of God toward us. "Oh, the love of God to send Jesus to take our sin! See Him hanging on that cross taking the wrath of God for you so you can be forgiven!" My heart ached. The power of God in that place was electric. My heart was screaming, "I need to repent, I need to repent!"

Finally, the call to get right with God came, and the song urged us to run to the mercy seat. Prostrate at the altar, I wept. I felt the Holy Spirit doing a very deep work. That evening I saw and experienced the power of God like never before in my life.

One thing I knew for sure — that my life and ministry would never be the same again. I had experienced the power of the gospel. I had experienced the power of the Holy Spirit. I was also keenly aware that my ministry up until that point was entertainment-centered and not cross-centered.

Since that October evening, I have been consumed with a desire to live in holiness and to preach a cross-centered gospel.

I had discovered that the power of God lies in the message of the Cross.

What follows is how that discovery has revolutionized how I preach the gospel.

INTRODUCTION

> "For I am not ashamed of the gospel, for it is the power of God for salvation to everyone who believes." (Romans 1:16)

A pastor contacted me the other day asking us to do some evangelism workshops. "Nothing we have done in evangelism seems to work," he said. "We are hoping that your method of preaching open-air will be what could work for us too."

So many Christians are desperate to find something that works, something they can do to get people saved and add members to their church. Their experience in evangelism has left them frustrated.

First of all, you must know this. Your effectiveness in evangelism lies in the power of the message and not in your great communication skills or creative methodology.

It is the gospel message itself that is the power of God for salvation.

> "For I am not ashamed of the gospel, for it is the power of God for salvation to everyone who believes." (Romans 1:16)

Your first step towards powerful evangelism is to clearly understand the message of the gospel.

So let's begin.

WHAT IS THE GOSPEL MESSAGE?

The gospel message has four essential parts. We can call them four columns.

Think of it as a chair with four legs. Each leg is necessary for the chair to function correctly. Remove a leg, and the chair will fall.

A building has four principal columns that sustain it. Remove just one column, and the whole building will collapse.

So it is with the four parts of the gospel message. Remove just one column of the message, and it becomes unstable and incomplete. Although each column is powerful in itself, all four columns are essential in presenting the complete gospel message in all of its power.

WHAT ARE THE FOUR COLUMNS OF THE GOSPEL MESSAGE?

1. **Law**. God's perfect Law reveals your **Problem** of sin.
2. **Eternity**. The focus on Eternity shows the terrible **Consequence** of your sin.
3. The **Cross**. Jesus' sacrifice on the Cross offers you a **Solution** to your problem.
4. **Repentance** and **Faith**. Repentance and Faith are required for you to Respond to the message and receive salvation.

The following chapters will explain each column and how all four columns work together powerfully to lead people to salvation.

CHAPTER ONE

The Problem

The Problem

I was 17 years old when I got my driver's license. I bought a 1974 Ford Mustang. (Okay, my mom bought it, and I made monthly payments to her.) One day while driving down Highway 64, I passed a car in a no-passing zone and found myself heading directly toward an oncoming vehicle. To avoid a head-on collision with the car, which happened to be a police car, I drove into the ditch on my left. The squad car pulled over with its lights flashing, and the policeman had to trudge down into the ditch to reach my car. I sheepishly rolled down my window as he asked me for my license. I had broken the law, and I knew immediately I had a huge problem.

All of us have a huge problem. We have broken God's Law.

COLUMN ONE

THE LAW

WHAT IS THE LAW?

Although the Old Testament ceremonial law no longer applies to us as Christians (which is why we can now eat bacon), God's moral law, the Ten Commandments, is still in effect.[3]

THE PURPOSE OF THE LAW

The Law reveals our sin problem.

> "Through the Law comes the knowledge of sin."[4]

---

3 Matthew 19:17
4 Romans 3:20

The Ten Commandments are like a mirror into your soul. As you gaze into the perfect Law of God, it reflects what is in your own heart — your rebellion, wickedness, idolatry, and pride.

The Ten Commandments clearly outline God's guidelines:

1. You shall have no other gods before Me.
2. You shall make no idols.
3. You shall not take the name of the Lord your God in vain.
4. Keep the Sabbath day holy.
5. Honor your father and your mother.
6. You shall not murder.
7. You shall not commit adultery.
8. You shall not steal.
9. You shall not bear false witness against your neighbor.
10. You shall not covet.

When you look at God's Commandments and then look at your own heart, your conscience will expose your guilt.

The Law brings conviction of sin.

The Law is written on every heart. That makes it a powerful ally.

> "They show that the work of the law is written on their hearts, while their conscience also bears witness, and their conflicting thoughts accuse or even excuse them."[5]

So even when speaking with people from other religions or no religion at all, you can know that the Law is written on their hearts. Therefore, when

---

5 Romans 2:15

CHAPTER ONE: THE PROBLEM

you aim at the heart and talk about God's moral Law, the Holy Spirit will awaken their conscience.

Jesus also promised that when the Holy Spirit came, He would convict people of sin, righteousness, and judgement.[6]

This is the Holy Spirit's job description among unbelievers. It is not our job to convict people of sin; it is His job. But as we talk about what sin entails, we are inviting the Holy Spirit to do His powerful work in their hearts and bring the conviction of sin that leads them to the Savior.

The Law leads us to Christ.

> "Therefore the law was our tutor to bring us to Christ,
> that we might be justified by faith."[7]

The Law was given the authority, as our guardian, schoolmaster, tutor, or teacher, to lead us to Christ. The Holy Spirit works alongside the Law of God to reveal our sin, destroy all of our hope in ourselves as good people, and lead us to the Savior, Jesus Christ, the only one who can rescue us from our sin.

Having a clear understanding of the purpose of the Law, you can see what a powerful tool this is in evangelism. Because the Law has been written on your heart, it has the power to show you your sin and lead you to Jesus.

In the next section, I will put the Law to work. What will stand out is that we have a serious problem. As I progress, you will discover seven deadly diseases. Keep alert for the multitude of illustrations used as they will come in handy while you evangelize. Also, be prepared for the Holy Spirit to reveal some of your own symptoms of these deadly diseases. You are about to have a deeper encounter with God as you see the power of His Law.

---

6 John 16:8
7 Galatians 3:24 (NKJV)

1. THE LAW REVEALS YOU ARE A SINNER
A Book in Heaven

The Book of Revelation speaks of men and women standing before God on Judgement Day when the books are opened and everyone is judged according to what they have done, good and bad.[8]

That means the book of your life records every time you have broken God's commandments in:

Thought	Word	Deed
• Jealousy	• Lies	• Stealing
• Hatred	• Criticism	• Rage
• Coveting	• Complaining	• Murder
• Lustful desires	• Gossiping	• Adultery
• Judgmental heart	• Blasphemy	• Sexual immorality

The problem is that the book of your life is filled with sin from cover to cover. We have all missed the mark and fallen short of God's standard of righteousness.[9] So then, on Judgement Day, what will happen? How will you remove the sin? How can you expect to enter heaven?

"The wages of sin is death."[10] Eternal death.

This is bad news!

---

8 Revelation 20:12.
9 Romans 3:23
10 Romans 6:23

2. THE LAW REVEALS YOU ARE GUILTY

Innocent or Guilty?

Let's say you have broken God's commands only 10 times a day: the toys you took away from your sister as a child revealing your selfishness, the lies you told your parents as a teenager, the unforgiveness that dwelt in your heart for years, the rebellious spirit, the lustful look, or the sex before marriage.

When you stand before the Judge of all the earth and have your life exposed before Him, will you be innocent or guilty of obeying His commands?

Ten sins per day over a life of 70 years would be 255,500 offenses against God, each one adding to the stack of fines you will have to pay on Judgement Day.

Feel free to compare yourself with others. The trouble is, the only sins you will have to give an account for are your own.

What will you do on that day when all you have done in secret comes to light[11] and the gavel comes down? Guilty! No lawyer. No one to defend you. No way to change the verdict.

You must remember, God is not bad. You are. God is only delivering justice as a good judge would. I received a $100 fine for passing in a no-passing zone, not because the judge was bad, but because I was a lawbreaker.

"Will not the judge of all the earth do rightly?"[12] God will bring about justice.

You haven't just sinned 10 times a day. The problem is you have broken God's Law in too many ways to count and you stand guilty.

This is bad news!

---

11 Luke 8:17
12 Genesis 18:25

3. THE LAW REVEALS YOU ARE DEAD

The Living Dead

Adam and his wife lived in a paradise called the Garden of Eden. They conversed and fellowshipped with God himself. They worked without sweat. They cultivated without weeds. They had only one rule from God to keep: Do not eat from the tree of the knowledge of good and evil.

God warned them if they ate the forbidden fruit they would surely die. But they ate and suddenly realized something *had* died.

Their innocence was dead, and shame filled their lives. Their special relationship with God was dead. They were expelled from the garden to walk with God no more in the cool of the night. The hope of reaching the tree of life back in the garden was dead, hence forfeiting their hope of living forever. Sin began its irreversible work of death in their physical bodies, and Adam and Eve eventually died.

Spiritually, they were cut off from their life support with God. This spiritual death is also seen when the Scripture says that *no one understands*. Why don't they understand? Because their spiritual understanding is dead. *No one seeks for God*. Why don't they seek him? They cannot, because they are dead. *No one does good, not even one*. Why not? The dead cannot do good.[13]

We are the living dead. Just as a dead corpse has a stench, so it is with the spiritually dead. Our lives reek of:

- Pride and arrogance
- Hatred
- Rebellion against God
- Critical attitudes
- Deception and cheating
- Ungratefulness

"You were dead in your trespasses and sins."[14]

The problem is the dead cannot raise themselves to life again. Not physically and not spiritually.

This is bad news!

---

13 Romans 3:10-12
14 Ephesians 2:1

PROBLEM

LAW

SINNER
GUILTY
DEAD
SLAVE

4. THE LAW REVEALS YOU ARE A SLAVE
Promises, Promises

> *When I was a young boy, my dad struggled with alcoholism. He would come home from a drinking binge and say to the family, "I promise I will never drink again." It was a promise he could not keep. Drink was stronger than he was, and eventually, my parents divorced. Years later, when I was in Bible college, I received a phone call from my dad. He had been depressed and suicidal, and in desperation he had called a pastor. As my dad sat in the pastor's office, he had a powerful encounter with Jesus and was born again. Soon afterwards, while sitting on the sofa in his living room, he called out to God, "You had the power to save my soul, now I need your power to set me free from alcohol." During that phone call, my dad shared how the Spirit of God came into the living room and in the blink of an eye, he was completely set free from alcoholism. He never took another drink for the rest of his life.*

Many of us also make promises we cannot keep.

- You want to stop reliving the abuse you suffered as a child, but you are a slave to bitterness and unforgiveness.
- You vow to stop looking at pornography, but you are a slave to lust.
- You want to treat your family better, but you just can't stop yelling at them because you are a slave to rage.

You are always making promises to change, but you just can't. You are chained to something more powerful than yourself.

> "Everyone who sins, is a slave to sin."[15]

The problem is that your evil nature makes demands, and you are quick to submit. The devil tempts, and you give in. The world beckons, and you follow. You are a slave, and you have no way of escaping.

This is bad news!

---

15 John 8:34

5. THE LAW REVEALS YOU ARE DIRTY
A Stain on Your Life

You hear the lament in people's voices as they confess regrets about things they did in life. They have a stain on their character. They feel dirty. If they could only have another chance.

For example, you always have to be right. You always have to have the last word. Your haughty spirit wouldn't think of ever asking forgiveness. Then your conscience accuses you of being unclean.

You lament the sexually transmitted disease you got because of your multiple sexual partners as you fed that demon of lust that could never be satisfied. You are dirty.

These are stains on your life, your conscience, and your reputation.

Perhaps if you do some good things, you can balance out the bad you have done? Perhaps God would take that into account? Yet even your acts of righteousness are as filthy rags before God,[16] contaminated by your pride and conceit.

> The problem is you have countless stains of sin on your life that you cannot remove, and this makes you dirty before a holy God.

This is bad news!

---

16 Isaiah 64:6

6. THE LAW REVEALS YOU ARE AN ENEMY OF GOD
My Will, Not Yours

When Adam and Eve disobeyed God by eating from the tree, in essence they were saying, "I know what you said, God, but I am going to do it my way instead! My will be done, not yours!"

As a result, they were banished from the presence of God and denied access to the tree of life.

When you choose your way over God's way, He calls you an enemy. This is a VERY strong word in the Bible.

- It is the same word used for the devil when the Bible talks of the enemy who sows the weeds.[17]
- It is the kind of enemy that is referred to in Colossians: "And although you were formerly alienated and hostile [an enemy] in mind, engaged in evil deeds."[18]
- It is explained in James, as well, "Do you not know that friendship with the world make you an enemy with God? Therefore whoever wishes to be a friend of the world makes himself an enemy of God."[19]

---

17 Matthew 13:39
18 Colossians 1:21
19 James 4:4

Why are we God's enemies? The short answer is because we rebel against and disobey all of His commands.

- "Love God with all your heart." Yet we love ourselves with all our heart.
- "Do not lie." Yet we lie all the time.
- "Live in purity." Yet we live in sexual immorality.
- "Do not covet." Yet we are full of greed and love for money.
- "Do my will." No! We will do our will!

Imagine an earthly kingdom with a benevolent king who has moral laws and cares for his kingdom. His subjects, however, disregard all that he says and live as they please, as if the king did not exist. They would be considered rebels and enemies.

C.S. Lewis wrote, "Fallen man is not simply an imperfect creature who needs improvement; he is a rebel who must lay down his arms."[20]

Jesus tells the story about a king who gave his servants three months' wages so they could invest the money and put it to work. But his subjects hated him and sent a delegation after him to say, "We don't want this man to be our king."[21] The response of the king was chilling.

---

20 Mere Christianity, Chapter 4, p. 59
21 Luke 19:14

CHAPTER ONE: THE PROBLEM

"But as for these enemies of mine, who did not want me to reign over them, bring them here and slaughter them before me."[22]

The problem is that one day you will stand before God as His enemy. What will you do on that day?

This is bad news!

---

22 Luke 19:27

7. THE LAW REVEALS YOU ARE UNDER HIS WRATH
It Is a Dreadful Thing

I am not sure what you expect God to do when you stand before Him as a sinner, full of guilt, spiritually dead, a slave to your sin, dirty, and as His enemy.

Perhaps you hope for mercy? But it will be too late. One day, the Master of the house will stand up and shut the door, and you will be left outside begging to get in.[23]

Rather than finding an open door to God's house, you will hear the verdict: "Depart from me all you workers of evil."[24]

How can you accuse God of being bad when the Scripture says it is because of our *own* hard and impenitent heart that we are storing up wrath for ourselves on the day of judgement?[25]

Why do we deserve His wrath?

God is holy and righteous, and He will destroy all who live in rebellion against Him. This is a strong warning for people who live in these kinds of sin:

• Immorality	• Evil desire	• Wrath
• Impurity	• Greed	• Malice
• Passion	• Anger	• Abusive speech[26]

The problem is that one day you will have to pay for your own sin and you will have to drink the cup of God's wrath. Where will you hide on that day? Will you call to the mountains and the rocks, "Fall on us and hide us from the face of Him who sits on the throne and from the wrath of the Lamb!"?[27]

It will be a dreadful thing to fall into the hands of the living God.[28]

This is bad news!

---

23 Luke 11:25
24 Matthew 7:23
25 Romans 2:5
26 Colossians 3:8-9
27 Revelation 6:16
28 Hebrews 10:31

REVIEW

Let's review the first column of the gospel message.

1. You have a serious problem, which is sin.

2. God's Law, the Ten Commandments, reveals your sin, brings conviction of sin, and shows you your need for a solution.

3. The bad news is that you are a sinner, guilty, spiritually dead, a slave to sin, dirty, an enemy of God, and under His wrath.

FINAL REMARKS

Having read this far, you have probably noticed by now the powerful effect of the Law in your own life. It is very likely that the Holy Spirit has convicted you of specific sins you have been harboring in your heart. Take advantage of this opportunity to repent and come to Jesus for forgiveness.

In the same way, when you use the commandments in evangelism, the Holy Spirit will convict others of their sin. He will reveal through the commandments that sin is sinful beyond measure.[29]

As you give practical examples of how we break God's Law, keep your eye open for conviction of sin among your listeners. It may look like this:

- They avoid eye contact.
- They become worried.
- They begin to cry.
- Their heads drop in shame.
- They stop justifying their sin. When the Law does its work, its purpose is to "stop (close) every mouth and hold the whole world accountable to God"[30].

---

29 Romans 7:13
30 Romans 3:19

- They confess their sin. This means agreeing with God that He is right and they are wrong.

Don't rush through this powerful tool. John Wesley, founder of the Methodist church, recommended that his preachers would preach the Law until they could visibly see conviction among the listeners. Many would cry out in anguish. It was then he would offer them a solution for the problem.[31]

Do not soft-pedal the gospel. When you play piano and use the "soft pedal," it is something that muffles, deadens, and reduces effect. You soft-pedal the gospel by not sharing the Law with people or by rushing through this vital step. Often, we want to protect people from feeling bad or guilty, but the conviction of sin is a beautiful gift from God to prepare people for repentance that, in turn, leads to salvation. Don't cheat them of this deep experience with God. The more they see the depth of their sin, the more they will see the greatness of Jesus' sacrifice, and the more they will love the Savior. He who is forgiven much, loves much.[32]

Do not dilute the gospel. To dilute is to make something weaker in force by modifying it or adding other elements to it. In Sweden, they have a fruit concentrate called SAFT. It is diluted by adding 4 cups of water to 1 cup of concentrate. I was not aware of this process when I first visited Sweden. One day, I poured myself a cup of concentrate and drank it. "Wow! Now that was powerful!" I thought. "How do they drink this stuff?" When sharing the gospel, people need to hear it in the concentrated form, at full strength, without diluting, so they will end up saying, "Wow! Now that was powerful!"

Do not dull the sword. A sword is only useful when sharp. By avoiding talking about sin, you dull the sword. The Law will cut through the listeners' excuses and justifications to awaken their conscience and prepare them for the solution to their sin problem.[33]

---

31 The Works of John Wesley, Volume 11, page 486-7
32 Luke 7:47
33 Hebrews 4:12

Where is the power of the Law?

Allow the full effect of the Law to do its work. Herein lies the power.

When you use the Law in evangelism:

1. You are aiming for the heart where God has written His law and the sinner's conscience will be awakened.[34]

2. The Holy Spirit will convict of sin and raise up God's standard of righteousness. [35]

3. God will show the sinner his great need and prepare him to seek a solution for his sin.[36]

When the full effect of the Law has been accomplished, the sinner should be asking, "What must I do to be saved?!"

> The bad news must be understood before the good news will be desired.

Before someone is willing to submit to surgery, radiation, and chemotherapy, they must first be aware of the bad news that they have cancer. A scan, a meeting with the oncologist, and the dreadful news will lead a patient to say, "What must I do to get rid of the cancer and be well? What solution do you offer me?" And so it will be when you take someone through the Law. They will see the bad news of their sin and seek a solution.

---

34 Romans 2:15
35 John 16:8
36 Galatians 3:24

TESTIMONY

David was watching the news of flooding on the TV in his barbershop. Giovani, a client from the homosexual community, walked in and commented on how it looked like the world was ending. Taking advantage of the opportunity, David asked him where he would go if the world did end? Would he be good enough to go to heaven? Had he obeyed God's commandments? As Giovani began to see his life reflected in the Ten Commandments, he recognized that he was guilty of lying, stealing, sexual immorality, and coveting what he didn't have. The conviction of sin grew so strong on him that he threw his arms around David's neck and fell to his knees sobbing and calling out, "What can I do?!" Giovani begged Jesus for forgiveness and a clean heart. David encouraged him to leave his old life behind, to begin meeting with other believers, and to tell others what Jesus had done for him. As he wiped the tears from his eyes, Giovani left the barbershop that day with peace in his heart and the opportunity for a new beginning.

CHAPTER TWO

The Consequence

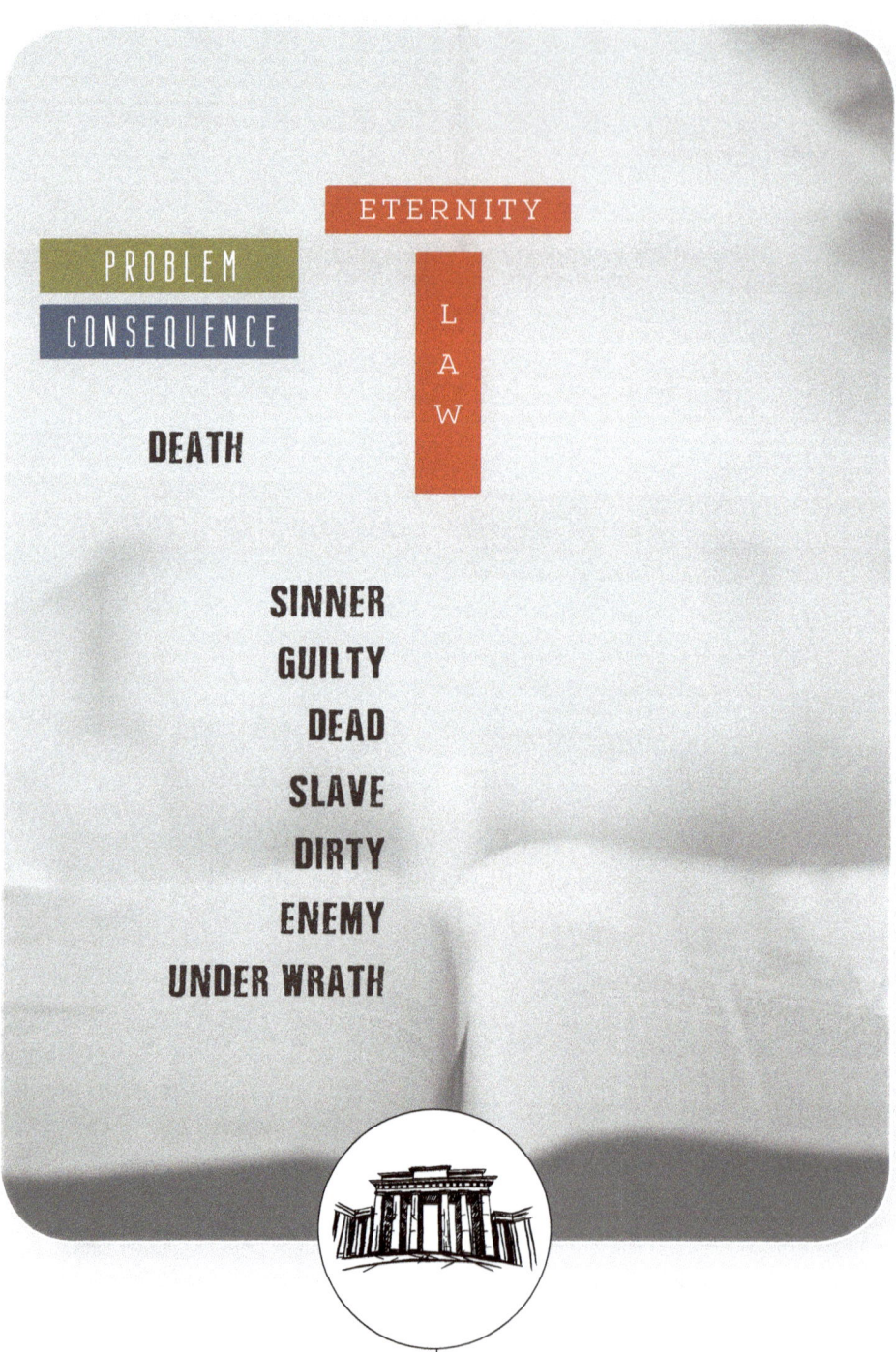

The Problem

A month after being pulled over by the police, I was in court standing before the judge. To my right sat the policeman that had issued me the traffic violation. The judge looked at me and said, "Jacob Francis Bock, on July 15th while driving on Highway 64, did you pass a car in a no-passing zone?" I glanced at the cop. What was I going to say? Of course I was guilty! "Yes, Your Honor, I did. I am so sorry. I promise I will never do it again." I was hoping he would overlook the fine. He did not. Now I had another problem. Who was going to pay my $100 fine?!

So the first column leaves you speechless and guilty before God. The second column will help you realize that the consequence for your sin is eternal death.

Before I get to the good news and the solution to the problem, you must understand the consequences of your sin.

When I stood before the judge, the evidence of my guilt was overwhelming. The question looming in my mind was, "What will my sentence be? How much will I have to pay? Will I go to jail?"

This is the final step of preparing the ground of the sinner's heart and getting him ready to hear what the Savior can do for him.

COLUMN TWO
ETERNITY

If someone close to you has died, chances are you have thought about eternity. In 2018, when my wife, Julie, was dying of cancer, we talked a lot about eternity. When people asked how she was doing, she would reply, "It is well with my soul." When evangelizing, she did not hide the fact that she was dying. She used her situation to warn people to be ready for the day we stand before God.[37]

---

37 Julie Bock went to heaven on April 18th, 2018.

Eternity is a mystery to us. Yet we do know that all people, regardless of race or religion, will face someday:

1. **Death**. Ten out of ten people born will die someday.
2. **Judgement.** After death the body is buried and the soul will be judged.
3. **Heaven or hell.** God has prepared two separate eternal destinations.

Eternity is written on every heart.

> "He has set eternity in the hearts of men." (Ecclesiastes 3:11)

There are two things written on every heart: God's Law and eternity. That shows the importance of including them in the gospel message.

What does the Bible say about eternity?

I. DEATH

Death Is Inevitable

> "It is appointed for man to die once, and after that to face judgement."[38]

Eating right and exercising can only improve your quality of life, but will not cause you to live forever. "And which of you by being anxious can add a single hour to his span of life?"[39]

Not thinking about death will not prevent it, and not preparing for it is foolish.[40]

Death Is an Enemy

The Bible identifies death as the last enemy to be conquered.[41] Jesus

---

38 Hebrews 9:27
39 Matthew 6:27
40 Luke 12:20
41 1 Corinthians 15:26

CHAPTER TWO: THE CONSEQUENCE 43

personally conquered death at His resurrection. And to His followers, He gave the promise that they would not suffer the second death,[42] that is, the lake of fire.

> Christians also have the promise of a physical resurrection of their own bodies, but until the final judgement, we will have to pass through the door of death.

Ways to Talk About Death

When you evangelize, you will need to introduce the topic of death. Though it is not often talked about, people are curious about what happens after we die. Here are a few examples of how we can broach the subject.

1. Do you think many or few will go to heaven when they die? This was a question someone asked of Jesus.[43] We can ask it too. Once they give their answer, you can follow up with, "Do you think you will be one of those that will go to heaven after dying?"

2. The statistic stands: "Ten out of ten people born in this city... will die someday." Then you follow up with, "Do you have any idea if God will let you into heaven when you die?"

3. Your life is like a vapor.[44] Use illustrations like vapor, clouds, and smoke to stress the brevity of life. Then talk about what follows.

After death comes the judgement.

---

42 Revelation 2:11
43 Luke 13:23
44 James 4:14

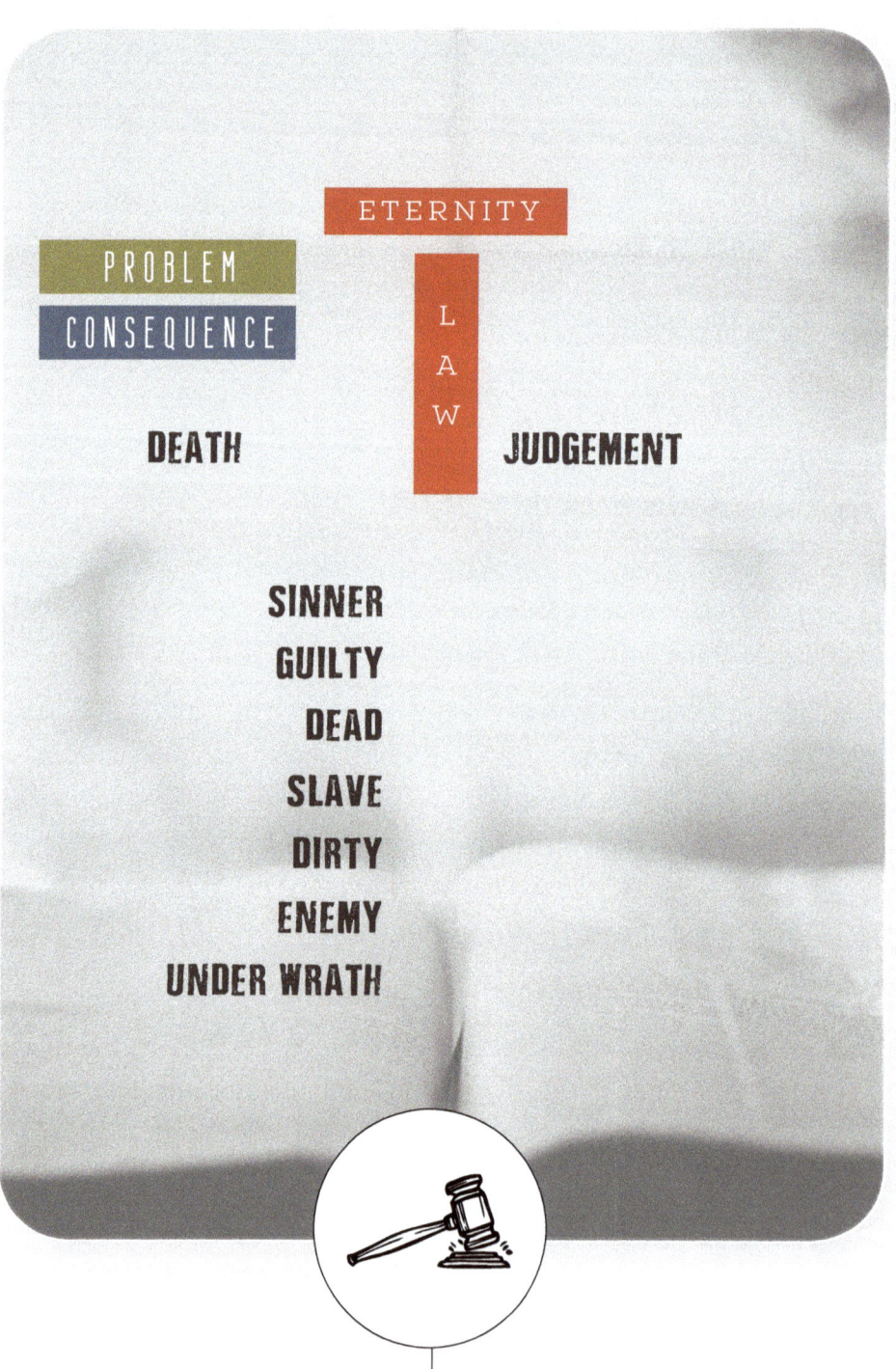

2. JUDGEMENT

When I stood before the judge to give an account for my reckless driving, it was very intimidating. There I stood with the judge, the accuser (the cop), the court reporter, and my guilt. After I promised the judge I would never do it again, the court reporter was busy recording everything that happened in the courtroom. The next day in my hometown newspaper it read, "Jacob Francis Bock was found guilty of passing in a no-passing zone. He received a fine of $100 and promised the court he would never do it again." Imagine how my friends razzed me the next day at school! How humiliating!

One day we will all stand before God to be judged. If you die forgiven, you will not have to pay for your sin, but you will be judged according to your works to determine your reward.

However, if you die in your sin, you will be judged according to everything written in your book to determine the full consequences of your sin.

Because eternity is written in your heart, there is this nagging sense that you might not get away with the evil you have done. "Vengeance is mine"[45] comes to mind, and you fear, and rightly so, as you must present your life before God.

Jesus told different stories to explain the kingdom of God to every class of society. In these stories, you can also see what the judgement will be like and what the consequences will be for those who die in their sins.

To the shepherd, He speaks of a separation between sheep and goats. "When the Son of Man comes in his glory, and all the angels with him, then he will sit on his glorious throne. Before him will be gathered all the nations, and he will separate people one from another as a shepherd separates the sheep from the goats. And he will place the sheep on his right, but the goats on the left."[46]

To the fisherman, He describes the fish being sorted and the bad ones cast away. "Again, the kingdom of heaven is like a net that was thrown into the

---

45 Romans 12:19
46 Matthew 25:31-33

sea and gathered fish of every kind. When it was full, men drew it ashore and sat down and sorted the good into containers but threw away the bad. So it will be at the end of the age. The angels will come out and separate the evil from the righteous and throw them into the fiery furnace. In that place there will be weeping and gnashing of teeth."[47]

To the farmer, He compares the wheat to the weeds. "Let both [weeds and wheat] grow together until the harvest, and at harvest time I will tell the reapers, 'Gather the weeds first and bind them in bundles to be burned, but gather the wheat into my barn.'"[48]

To the wedding guest who arrived totally unprepared, He recounts the drastic measures that were taken. "But when the king came in to look at the guests, he saw there a man who had no wedding garment. And he said to him, 'Friend, how did you get in here without a wedding garment?' And he was speechless. Then the king said to the attendants, 'Bind him hand and foot and cast him into the outer darkness. In that place there will be weeping and gnashing of teeth.'"[49]

The basic idea of the judgement is that there will be a separation of people. Some have entrance into heaven, the others will be cast away to hell. Now I have a confession I want to make. As I wrote the previous sentence about hell, I was tempted to soften it and say, "Some have entrance in heaven, the *others do not*." Words like hell, lake of fire, and eternal torment sound so harsh and shocking. Well, hell is a shockingly harsh place. If you try to imagine what hell will be like, understand that it is probably worse than you imagine. Jesus didn't shy away from using these words, so neither should you. Just do so with a loving heart.

The Importance of <u>Your</u> Book

We know one day the books will be opened.[50] The main issue on

---

47 Matthew 13:47-50
48 Matthew 13:30
49 Matthew 22:11-13
50 Revelation 20:12,13

Judgement Day has to do with your book and what is written in it. Your life will be judged according to the Law of God. Any sin found in your book excludes you from heaven, even if only one sin is found. "For whoever keeps the whole law but fails in one point has become guilty of all of it."[51]

The Two Possible Verdicts

On that day, you will hear Jesus say one of two things:

1. "COME, you who are blessed by my Father, inherit the kingdom prepared for you from the foundation of the world."[52]

Imagine standing before Jesus with a sin-free book and hearing Him call you by name, "Come, Jacob!" What a day of rejoicing that will be! The doors of heaven open wide, you receive your crown of life, and enter into the joy of the Lord to the place He prepared for you!

Or you may hear:

2. "DEPART from me, you cursed, into the eternal fire prepared for the devil and his angels."[53]

Oh, the dread! What a terrible thing to fall into the hands of a living God![54]

Oh, the regret! If only you would have turned from your sin and run to Christ for forgiveness, but now it is too late.

"Oh, the weeping and gnashing of teeth when you see others enter and you are cast out!"[55]

Look! Here come the servants to execute the sentence delivered down from the judgement seat of God. "Bind him hand and foot, and cast him into the outer darkness; there will be the wailing and the gnashing of teeth."[56]

Woe to the one that hears the word: "Depart"!

---

51 James 2:10
52 Matthew 25:34
53 Matthew 25:41
54 Hebrews 10:31
55 Luke 13:28
56 Matthew 22:13

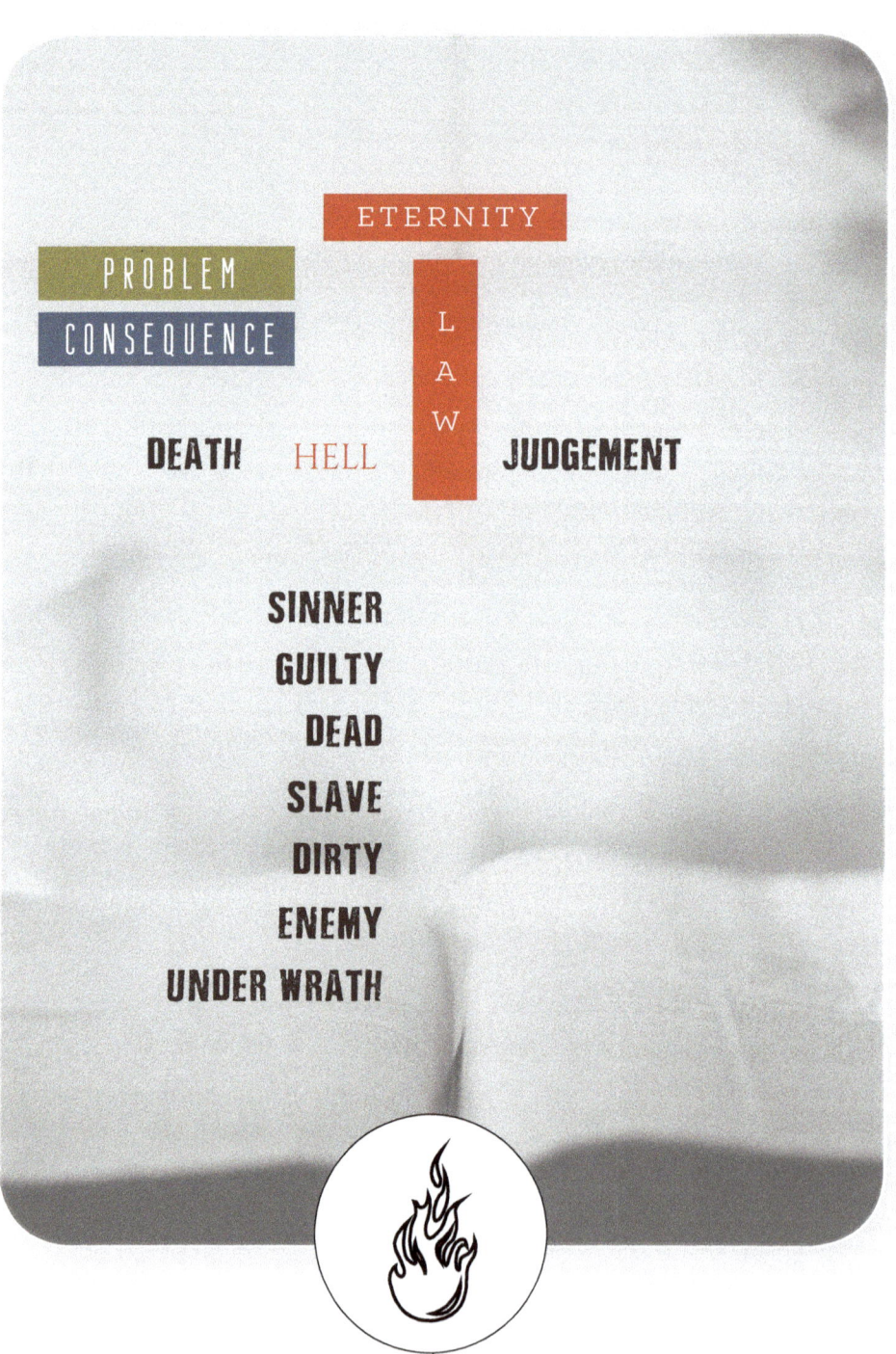

3. HELL

> "For the gate is wide and the way is easy that leads to destruction, and those who enter by it are many."[57]

Sadly, most people die in their sins because they prefer their life, their sin, their religion, or their reputation over repentance and submission to Christ.

The majority of what we know about hell is what Jesus told us. The fact that He spoke three times more about this place of torment than He did about heaven should tell you how important this was to Him. If warning about judgement and hell was important to Jesus, it should be important to you, too, as you share the gospel message.

What Is Hell?

Many people say we are experiencing hell right here on earth. And in part, they are right, because we experience some of the consequences of sin here on earth. There is suffering; there are tears; there are broken relationships; there is anguish and loneliness. But we also experience a little bit of heaven on earth. We enjoy friendship and love; we appreciate beauty and have hope for the future. When we are hungry, we can eat. When we are thirsty, we can drink. But these are gifts from God that will not be in hell.

People say they will enjoy partying with their friends in hell. But there will be no friends in hell, only loneliness and darkness. There will be no enjoyment in hell, only suffering and remorse.

So how will hell be different from what we are experiencing on earth?

- Hell is the total absence of God and everything good because "every good gift and every perfect gift is from above, coming down from the Father of lights."[58] But because God is not there, there will be nothing good in hell.

---

57 Matthew 7:13
58 James 1:17

- There is no love in hell because God is love, and He is not there.[59]
- There is no goodness in hell because God is good, and He is not there.[60]
- There is no hope in hell because God is the God of hope, and He is not there.[61]
- There is no life in hell because Jesus is the life, and He is not there.[62]
- There is no water in hell because Jesus gives living water, and He is not there.[63]
- There is no nourishment in hell because Jesus is the Bread of Life, and He is not there.[64]
- There is only darkness in hell because Jesus is the Light of the World, and He is not there.[65]
- There is no way out of hell because Jesus is the door, and He is not there.[66]

> "They will suffer the punishment of eternal destruction, away from the presence of the Lord and from the glory of his might."[67]

Hell is just horrendous. No one enjoys thinking about it. No one enjoys preaching about it. No one can understand how wretched a place it really is. But before I leave this brief overview of hell, you must understand:

God does NOT want you to go there.

- His desire is that all come to repentance to avoid this place of destruction.[68]
- Hell was created for the devil and his angels, not for people.[69]

---

59 1 John 4:8
60 Mark 10:18
61 Luke 16:26; Romans 15:13
62 John 14:6
63 Luke 16:24; John 7:38
64 John 6:35
65 John 8:12
66 John 10:7
67 2 Thessalonians 1:9
68 2 Peter 3:9
69 Matthew 25:41

CHAPTER TWO: THE CONSEQUENCE

- The Cross is the proof that God wants to spare you from that place.[70]

Hell is your choice; you are without excuse.

- There are two paths to eternity, the wide and the narrow. You can choose the narrow path that leads to life, or you can choose the wide path that leads to destruction.[71]
- Some of you are like the five brothers of the rich man in hell, who had the Law and the prophets to warn them, but did not listen.[72]
- God's desire was to gather you, as a hen gathers its chicks, but you would not let Him.[73]
- In the end, those who go to hell will only receive what they have chosen all of their lives — to live without God and have it their own way.

C.S. Lewis said: "There are only two kinds of people in the end: those who say to God, 'Your will be done' and those to whom God says, in the end, 'Your will be done.' All that are in hell, choose it."[74]

"How dreadful!" you say. Yes, it is. If it wasn't for the fact that "God so loved the world," hell would be your eternal destination. God is not willing that any perish. He desires all to come to repentance and have heaven as their eternal home.[75]

Yet Jesus said there will be few who will enter heaven. "For the gate is narrow and the way is hard that leads to life, and those who find it are few."[76]

Now let's take a look at what heaven will be like.

---

70 1 John 3:16
71 Matthew 7:13
72 Luke 16:31
73 Luke 13:34
74 The Great Divorce, page 75
75 2 Peter 3:9
76 Matthew 7:14

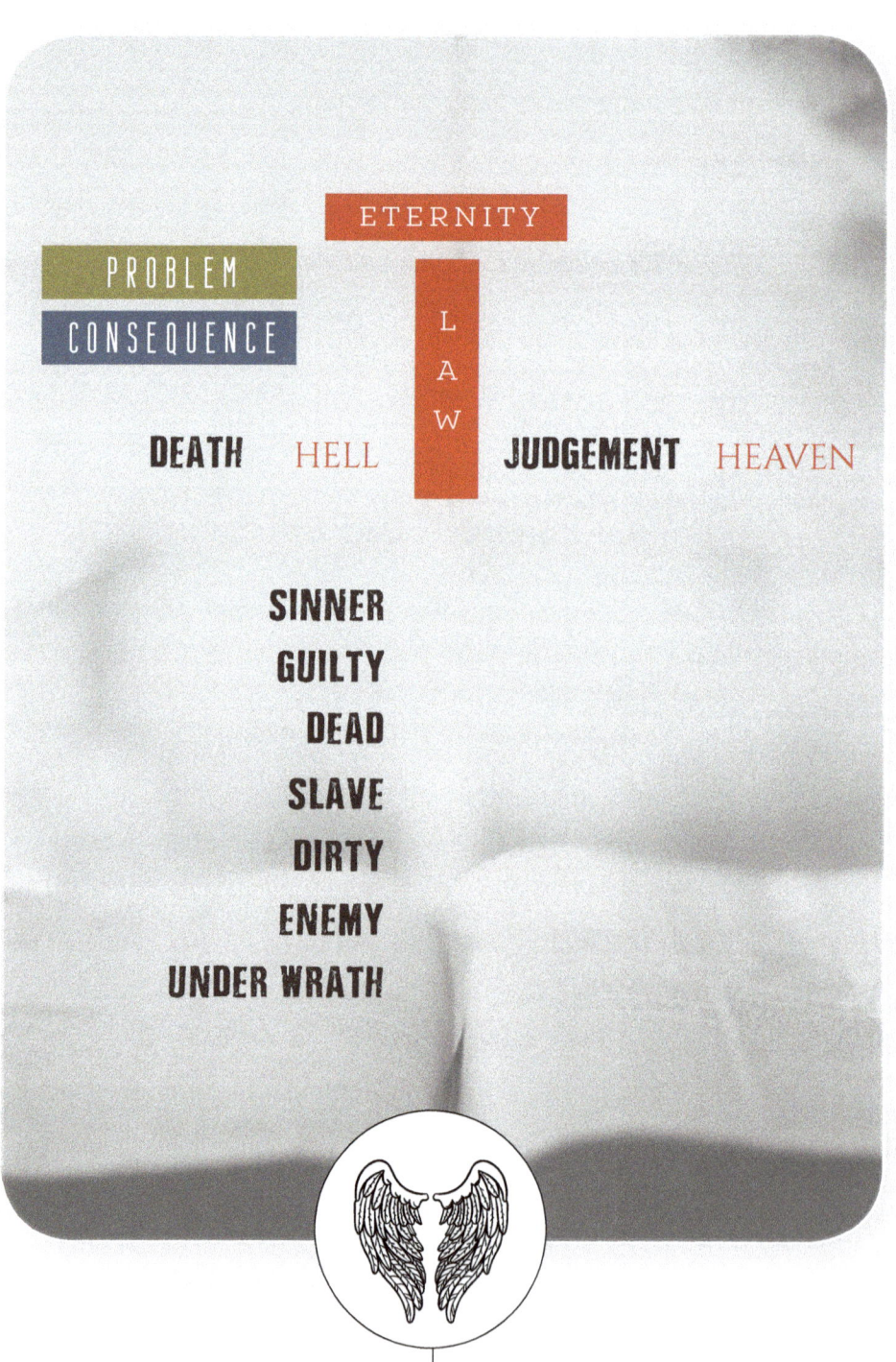

4. HEAVEN

What Is Heaven?

Heaven is God's home, a permanent place where God's presence resides. Because God is there, everything good is also there. There will be love, joy, peace, goodness, purity, and hope. You will be able to enjoy beauty, fellowship, and life to the fullest.

The majority of what we know about heaven we learn from Jesus and the Apostle John. Jesus said He would prepare a place for you there. John described heaven as the new Jerusalem, a city with streets of gold, rivers of living water, and the tree of life. There you will see loved ones who had believed, the angels of God, and best of all, you will see Jesus face to face in all of His glory!

In heaven you will NOT experience sin, nor any of its consequences. There will be no sickness, no death, no tears, no fear, no loneliness, and no depression. You will be forever free of the temptation, accusations, and condemnation of the devil and his demons.

Once you are in Christ, you become a citizen of heaven, and your desire is to be there with your Lord and Savior.

REVIEW

Let's review the second column of the gospel message.

By talking about eternity, the sinner is reminded of his imminent death and the certainty of being judged by God, while still in his sin. Judgement and hell are explained, so he is fully aware of the consequences.

When the Holy Spirit has done His work using the Law and eternity, the sinner should be desperate for a solution to his sin problem. Now the Cross will make sense to the sinner and reveal God's solution for him.

FINAL REMARKS

Where is the power in speaking of eternity?

1. Because the Holy Spirit convicts of the Day of Judgement, as you include that in your evangelism message, you invite Him to do His work and bring the sinner face to face with the consequences of his sin.[77]

2. Because God has placed eternity in the hearts of men,[78] as you speak of what happens after death, you are inviting the Holy Spirit to penetrate the heart of stone and awaken the indifferent sinner to face eternity.

> If you avoid talking specifically about death, judgement, heaven, and hell in evangelism, you have taken away one of the greatest tools of the Holy Spirit to warn the sinner of the terrible consequences of his sin.

When the Holy Spirit reveals the reality of the pending judgement and its consequences, He prepares the sinner to receive the good news.

---

77 John 16:8
78 Ecclesiastes 3:11

TESTIMONY

Jorge grew up in church and even became a youth leader. When he was 16, he was electrocuted while swimming and actually died. Before being resuscitated, he experienced deep fear about where he would spend eternity. A few years later, he went to Spain on a mission trip and became involved with ONTHEREDBOX. God began to confront him about his sins of pride, stealing, and lustful thoughts. Soon afterwards, he had a dream about hell, which led him to fall to his knees and cry out to God for forgiveness. He completely surrendered his life to Jesus then and experienced freedom from his sin. Jorge became so passionate about sharing about Jesus that he went on to raise up many evangelism teams in Mexico and Latin America to help others change their eternal destiny from hell to heaven.

CHAPTER THREE

The Solution

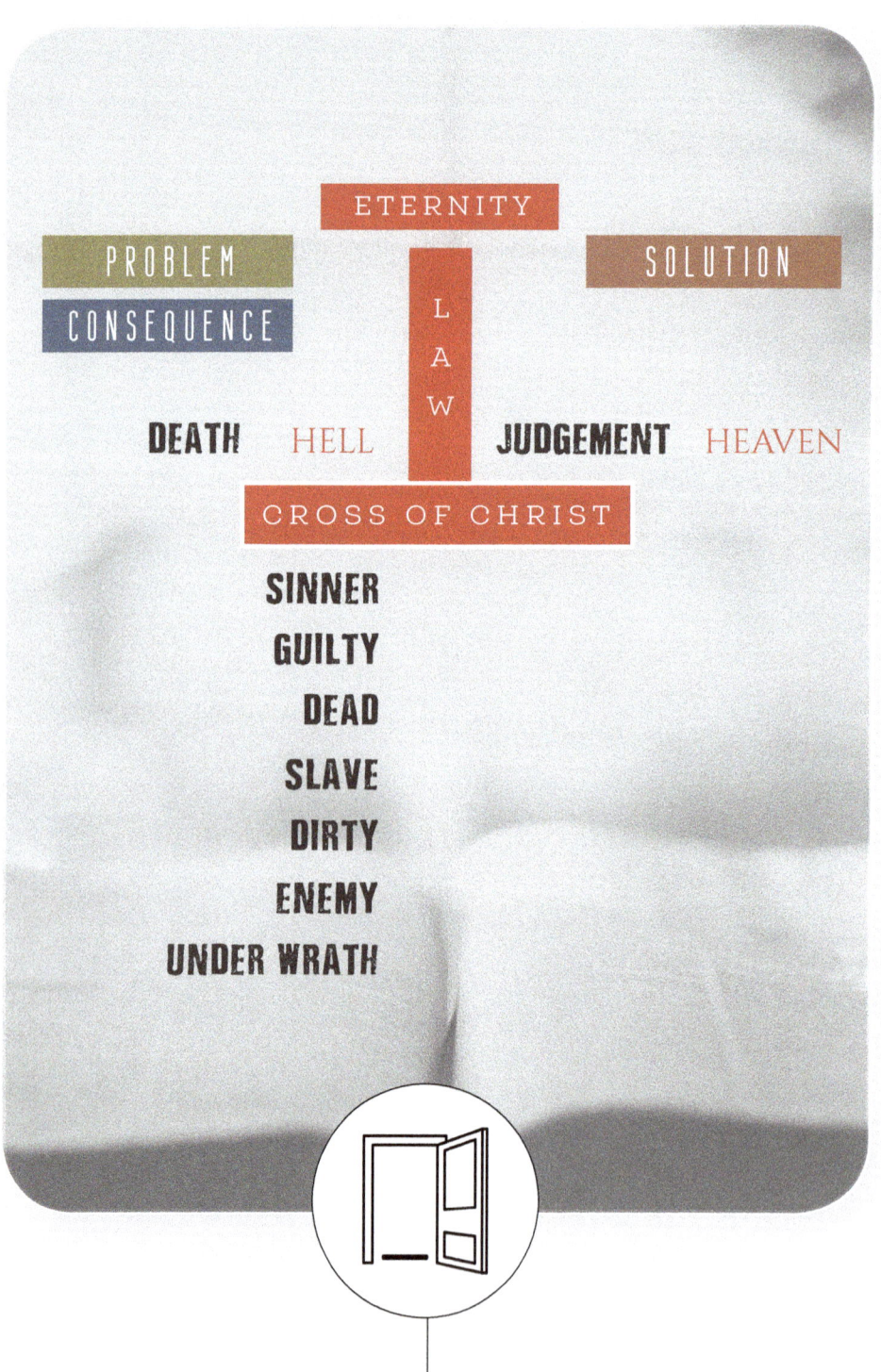

CHAPTER THREE: THE SOLUTION

I wish my traffic violation story had a better solution. I was handed the $100 fine and told to pay it. My parents would not pay it for me, nor would my best friend. I did not have the money, so I had to earn it by cleaning out all the manure in the chicken barn. It took me 20 hours of hard (and smelly) work to pay off the fine. How I wished someone would have stepped in to pay it for me!

The fines I owed for my sin were infinitely greater than the fine for my traffic ticket. So the solution Jesus offered me was infinitely greater too. Because He knew I could never work to pay for all of my sin, He chose to pay it for me. This is grace.

This is the message of the Cross, which offers us an incredible solution for our terrible problem and consequences.

As we look into the mirror of God's perfect Law, we are left speechless and guilty before God. Then, as we face eternity, the fear of God comes upon us as we realize the consequence for our sin is eternal death.

At this point, we should be desperate for a solution and cry out, "What must I do to be saved?"[79]

In the third column, Jesus Christ offers us a pardon for our sin and an open door to heaven.

---

79 Acts 16:30

COLUMN THREE
THE CROSS OF CHRIST

"For God so loved the world that he sent his only son." (John 3:16)

When God sent Jesus, He sent Him to be your substitute. He was sent to die in your place. He became the "Lamb of God that takes away the sin of the world."[80] He died so that He might clothe you in His righteousness and make you presentable before God the Father.

> Jesus knew full well your problem and the terrible consequences awaiting you. That is why He came to save you.

Through Jesus' death and resurrection, He proved that He could eliminate your sin and change all the bad news into good news.

Earlier, we took a hard look at the seven diseases that sin causes in our lives. It was all bad news. Now let's look at the atonement, that is, the good news of the seven main provisions Jesus won for you on the cross.

---
80 John 1:29

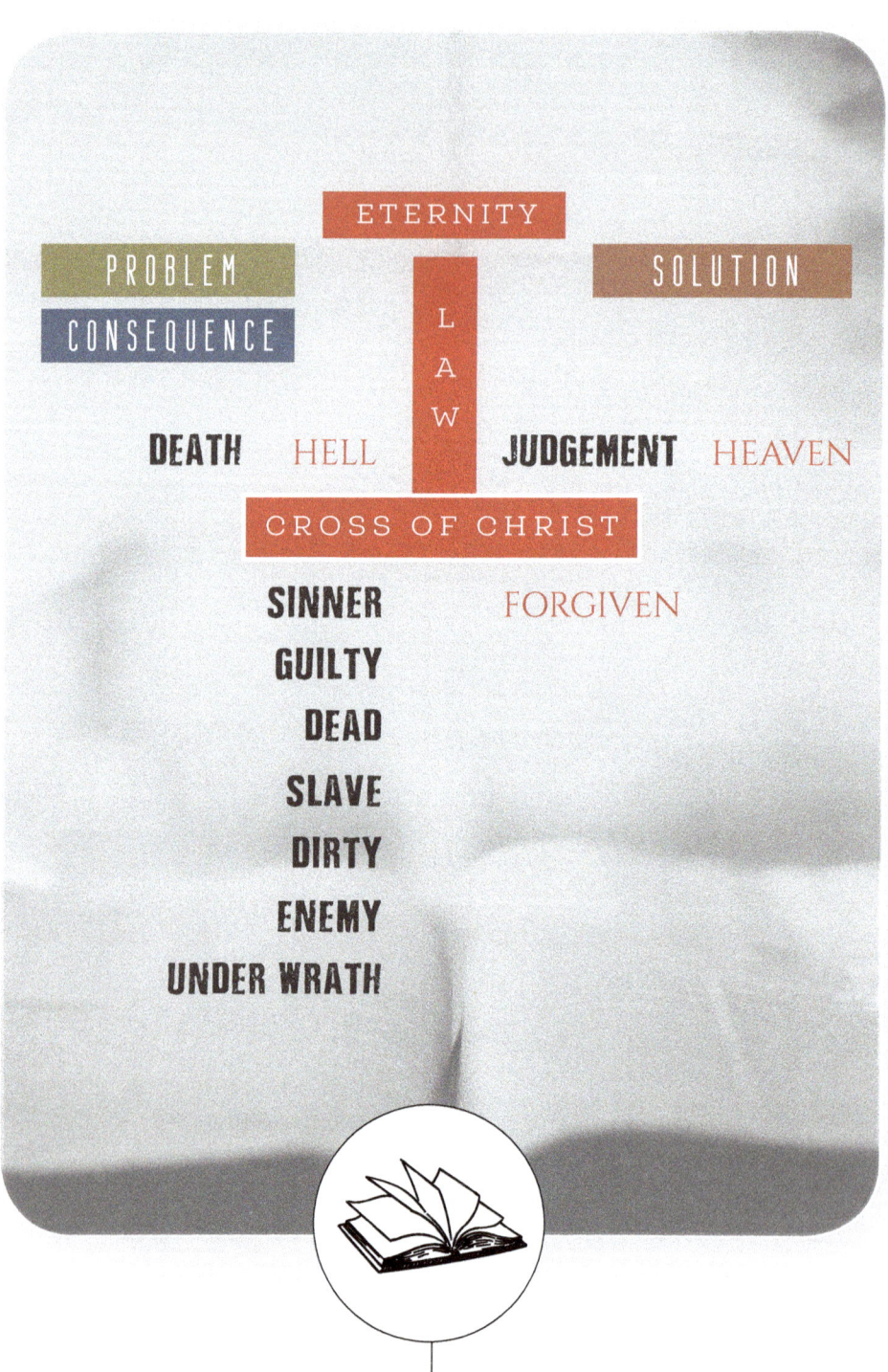

CHAPTER THREE: THE SOLUTION

1. FORGIVEN – JESUS TAKES YOUR PLACE

> "But God shows his love for us in that while we were still sinners, Christ died for us." (Romans 5:8)

Here are four things Jesus knows:

1. All of the sins written in the book of your life.
2. The payment for sin is death, hell, and the wrath of God.
3. On Judgement Day, you are slated to pay for your own sin.
4. You have no hope of saving yourself — unless you find a substitute!

Jesus will now deal with your sin problem. This is how He does it.

> "For our sake he made him to be sin who knew no sin, so that in him we might become the righteousness of God."[81]

On the cross, Jesus took the sin from your book upon Himself and "he was smitten by God, and afflicted. But he was wounded for our transgressions; he was crushed for our iniquities."[82]

Then by His resurrection, He proved He had the power to forgive the sinner.

The sinless one for the sinner. Jesus took your sin in order to offer you His forgiveness. This is good news!

Substitution. One takes the place of another or does what the other person cannot do for Himself.

---

81 2 Corinthians 5:21
82 Isaiah 53:4-5

TESTIMONY

As a young girl, Julie thought she was one of the good kids. But when she was only 10 years old, she was listening to someone talk about how Jesus came to save sinners. She got a glimpse of her own heart, and saw it was full of sin from all of the lies she had told, the many times she had stolen from her sister, and her pride for thinking she was so much better than everyone else. That day she fell to her knees and said, "Jesus, you came to save sinners. I am a sinner. Forgive me and change me!" When she stood up, something was different inside of her. She knew Jesus had forgiven her. From that day on, Julie lived to follow the one who had paid for all of her sin.

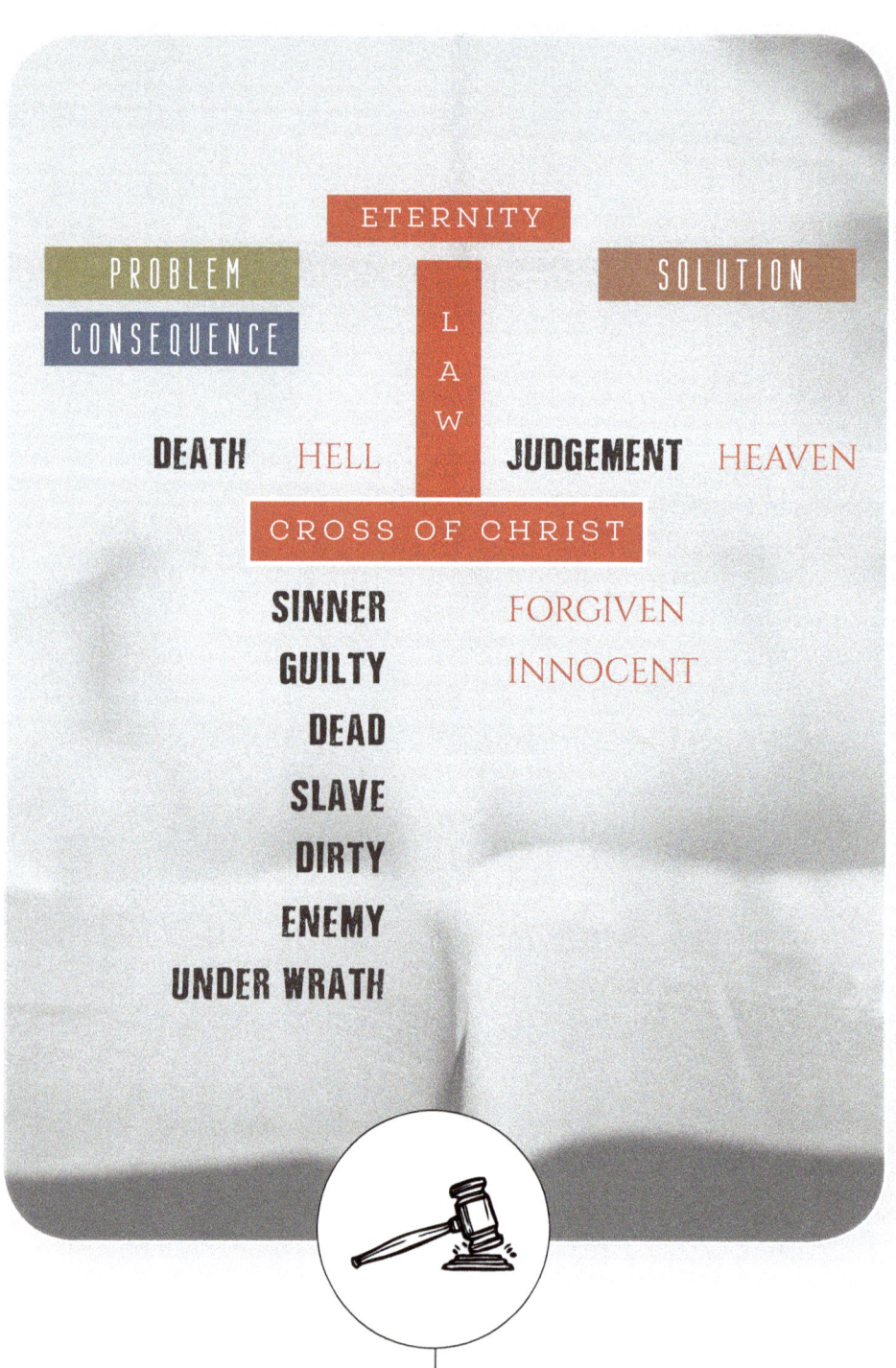

2. INNOCENT – JESUS JUSTIFIES YOU

> "Therefore, since we have been justified by faith, we have peace with God through our Lord Jesus Christ." (Romans 5:1)

Here are three things Jesus knows:

1. The number of times you have broken His Law.
2. Your verdict on Judgement Day will be guilty.
3. You have no possibility of erasing your own guilt — unless you find a substitute!

Jesus voluntarily takes your sin and guilt, and on the cross receives the verdict of guilty. He pays the price for your guilt and offers you His righteousness.

The innocent for the guilty. Jesus takes your guilt so He can give you His innocence. This is good news!

Justification. It is God's response to genuine faith where He simultaneously forgives our sin, declares our legal standing "perfectly sinless," and gives us the credit for the righteous life Jesus lived.

TESTIMONY

Juan Carlos assumed he would get into heaven because he considered himself a good person. He was surprised to discover one day that when he looked at God's Ten Commandments, he saw that he was guilty of stealing things that didn't belong to him, of lustful thoughts as he consumed pornography, and of hatred towards people who had offended him. The weight of that guilt was too heavy for him to carry. When a friend told him that Jesus died to pay for his sin, Juan Carlos prayed and asked Jesus to forgive him of his sin and take away all of his guilt. He was amazed and grateful as the weight of his sin disappeared, erased by Jesus' forgiveness!

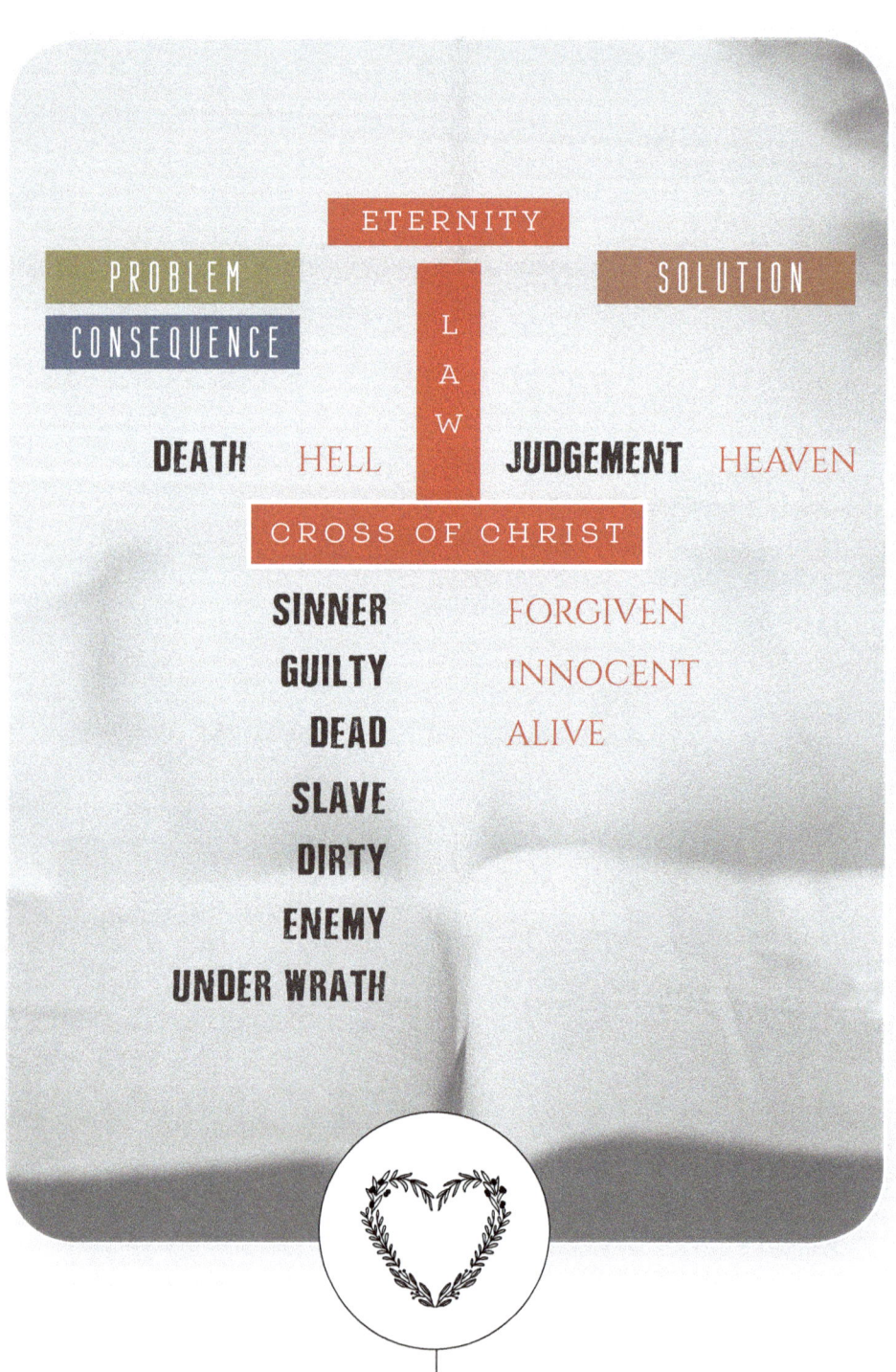

3. ALIVE – JESUS REGENERATES YOU

> "But God, being rich in mercy, because of the great love with which he loved us, even when we were dead in our trespasses, made us alive together with Christ – by grace you have been saved." (Ephesians 2:4-5)

Here are six things Jesus knows:

1. You are spiritually dead because of your sin.
2. Your sinful nature runs your life.
3. You don't have desires to live in holiness.
4. Your life feels empty and void.
5. On Judgement Day you will experience the second death, the lake of fire.
6. You have absolutely no hope of raising yourself from the dead — unless you find a substitute!

Jesus came that you might have life.[83] When He was nailed to the cross, He bore the penalty of your sin, namely death.

> "Jesus, crowned with glory and honor because of the suffering of death, so that by the grace of God he might taste death for everyone."[84]

Jesus conquered death and has the power to infuse you with His life, with His divine nature.

The living for the dead. Jesus took your death so He could give you His life. This is good news!

Regeneration. It is the infusion of God's divine nature that brings new spiritual life and is confirmed by genuine fruit.

---

83 John 10:10
84 Hebrews 2:9

TESTIMONY

I (Jacob) grew up in the church, so I had a knowledge of God. Even though I had said the sinner's prayer numerous times, nothing ever changed in my life. On Sundays I was a saint, and on weekdays I was a devil. At a Christian youth camp the Holy Spirit showed me my sin — my sexual impurity, lying to my parents, selfishness, and the list went on. I knew in that moment that I was going to hell. I cried out to Jesus to save me, and I fully surrendered to him. I immediately sensed the infusion of His Spirit. It was like putting a tea bag in hot water and the tea infusing all of the water. So when the Holy Spirit infused me, everything changed! I was born again. Jesus regenerated me.

4. FREE — JESUS REDEEMS YOU

> "He has delivered us from the dominion of darkness and transferred us to the kingdom of his beloved Son, in whom we have redemption, the forgiveness of sin." (Colossians 1:13-14)

Here are four things Jesus knows:

1. You have given yourself over to sin.
2. You are a slave to sins stronger than yourself.
3. On Judgement Day you will appear before God yoked to sin.
4. You have no hope of setting yourself free — unless you find a substitute!

You were given God's Law to obey, but instead you obeyed the lusts of your own flesh. You chose your own will rather than His. Therefore, you became a slave to sin.

Jesus also knew that if He sets you free, you will be free indeed.[85] So to purchase your freedom, He paid the price for your sin. He paid with His life. His life for yours.

The free man for the slave. Jesus took the bondage of your sin to offer you His freedom. This is good news!

Redemption. The purchase of something that had been lost by the payment of a ransom.

---

85 John 8:36

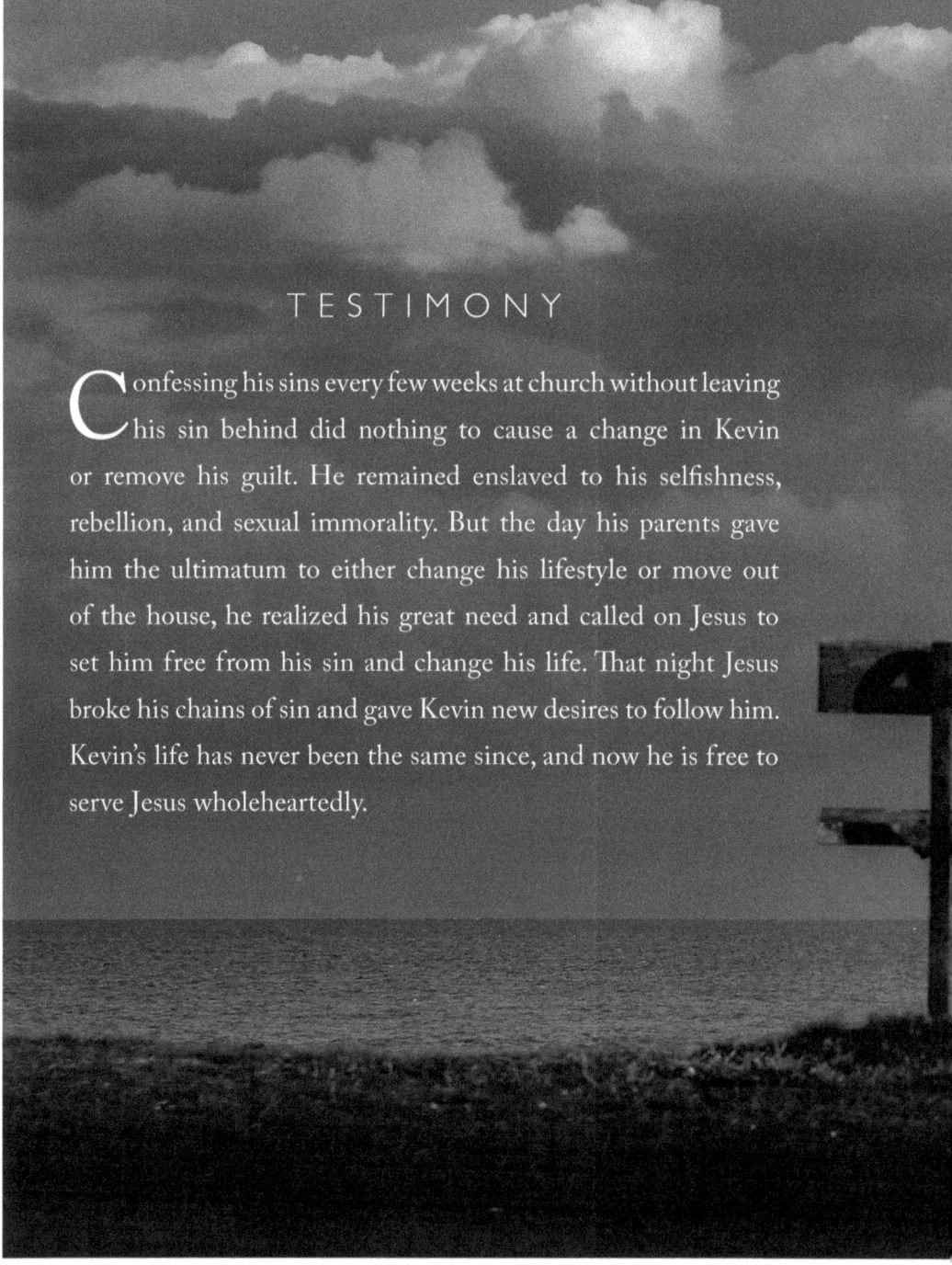

TESTIMONY

Confessing his sins every few weeks at church without leaving his sin behind did nothing to cause a change in Kevin or remove his guilt. He remained enslaved to his selfishness, rebellion, and sexual immorality. But the day his parents gave him the ultimatum to either change his lifestyle or move out of the house, he realized his great need and called on Jesus to set him free from his sin and change his life. That night Jesus broke his chains of sin and gave Kevin new desires to follow him. Kevin's life has never been the same since, and now he is free to serve Jesus wholeheartedly.

CHAPTER THREE: THE SOLUTION

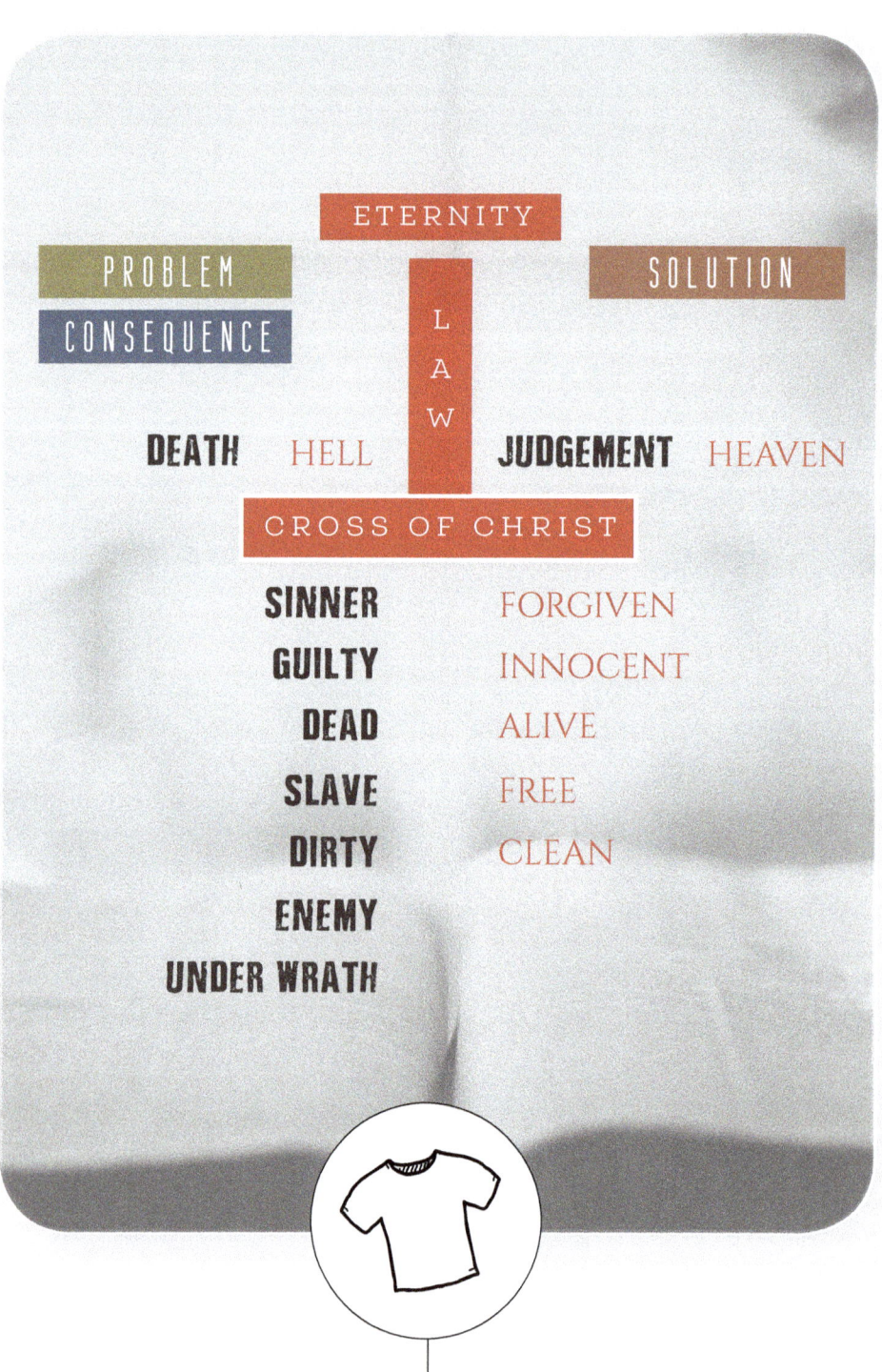

5. CLEAN – JESUS SANCTIFIES YOU

> "But now that you have been set free from sin and have become slaves of God, the fruit you get leads to sanctification and its end, eternal life."
> (Romans 6:22)

Here are six things Jesus knows:

1. Your conscience is stained with sin.
2. You find it impossible to live in holiness (separated from the world and set apart for God).
3. You have more of the image of sin on your character than the image of Christ.
4. Your righteousness is as dirty rags before Him.
5. On Judgement Day, you will stand before God covered in the filth of your sin.
6. You have no hope of removing the stain of sin by yourself — unless you find a substitute!

Jesus took your impurity, filth, selfishness and all your sin upon Himself when He died. And what He purchased was your sanctification.

> The clean for the unclean. Jesus took your filth so He could give you His purity. This is good news!

Sanctification. Sanctification took place the instant God (1) set us apart at conversion when (2) we began the lifelong process of putting flesh and bone on holiness until (3) our complete sanctification is fully realized when Christ returns.

TESTIMONY

Cinthia was active in her church, graduated from a Bible School, and even became involved in street evangelism. But one day, as she sat in an evangelism workshop that detailed our sin problem and why it was necessary for Jesus to die on the cross, a heavy conviction of sin came upon her. It lasted for two months, and during that time she saw a vision of herself immersed in the filth of her pride and deception. Then a hand reached into the filth, pulled her out, hosed off the mud and slime, and made her clean. This led her to deeply repent of all of her sin, and she was filled with gratitude to Jesus for His forgiveness. Her encounter with Jesus has compelled her to passionately share the gospel with others so they can also experience Jesus' cleansing and forgiveness.

CHAPTER THREE: THE SOLUTION

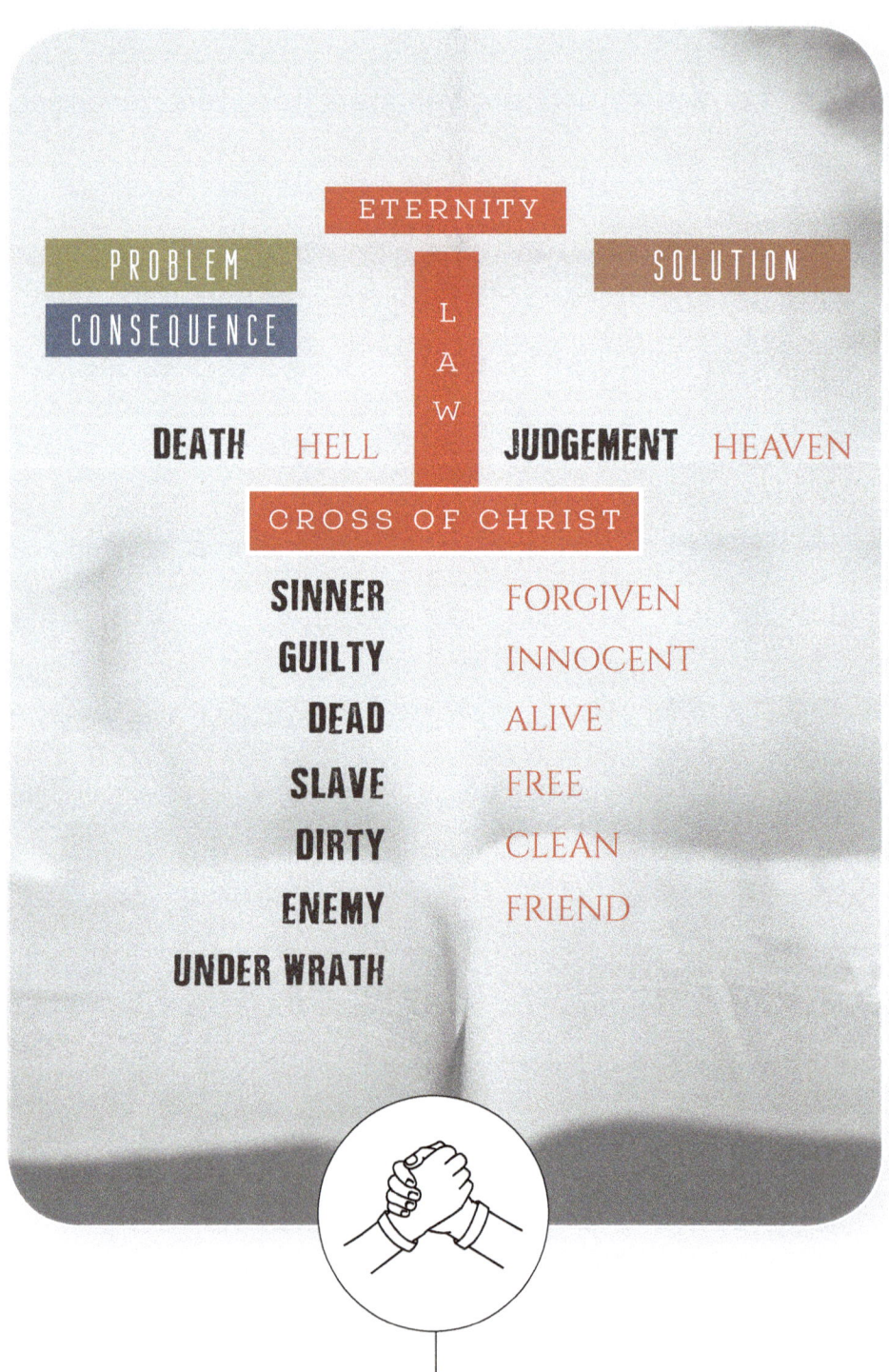

6. FRIEND – JESUS RECONCILES YOU

> "For if while we were enemies we were reconciled to God by the death of his Son, much more now that we are reconciled, shall we be saved by his life." (Romans 5:10)

Here are five things Jesus knows:

1. When God gave you His Law, you chose to disobey.
2. As a friend of the world, you make yourself an enemy of God.
3. When you stand before God on Judgement Day, you will be regarded as His enemy.
4. His enemies will be cast out of His kingdom.
5. There is no hope, by your own efforts, for reconciliation — unless you find a substitute!

Jesus wants to reconcile you to God. The only way for this to happen is for Him to take the rebellion from within your heart, take your sin, and die in your place. Jesus became God's enemy when He took all of your sin on the cross and the Father turned His back on Him. That's when Jesus said, "My God, my God, why have you forsaken me?!"[86] Jesus became God's enemy so you could become His friend.

The friend dies for the enemy. This is good news!

Reconciliation. Jesus removes the sin and hatred which separates us from God and bridges the gap so our relationship will continue throughout eternity.

---

86 Mark 15:34

TESTIMONY

Arnold was raised in Berlin, Germany, during the time when an impenetrable wall separated East Germany from West Germany. The nation, the city, and countless families were separated by the wall until it finally fell in 1989, uniting the country once again. Growing up in church, Arnold knew his sin was like a wall that separated him from God, and he tried hard to get rid of the barrier of sin. He repeated the sinner's prayer, got baptized, attended every church meeting possible, and confessed his sin, but he still felt far from God. One day he prayed, "God, I don't feel you love me, and I haven't experienced your forgiveness. If the Cross has anything to do with me, please show me." And God did just that. Only a few months later, during the Lord's Supper, Arnold finally understood that Jesus took his place on the cross and was punished for his sin. He chose to fully rely on what Jesus had done, turned to Jesus, and turned his back on sin. That day God broke down the wall of separation, and Arnold's life radically changed.

CHAPTER THREE: THE SOLUTION

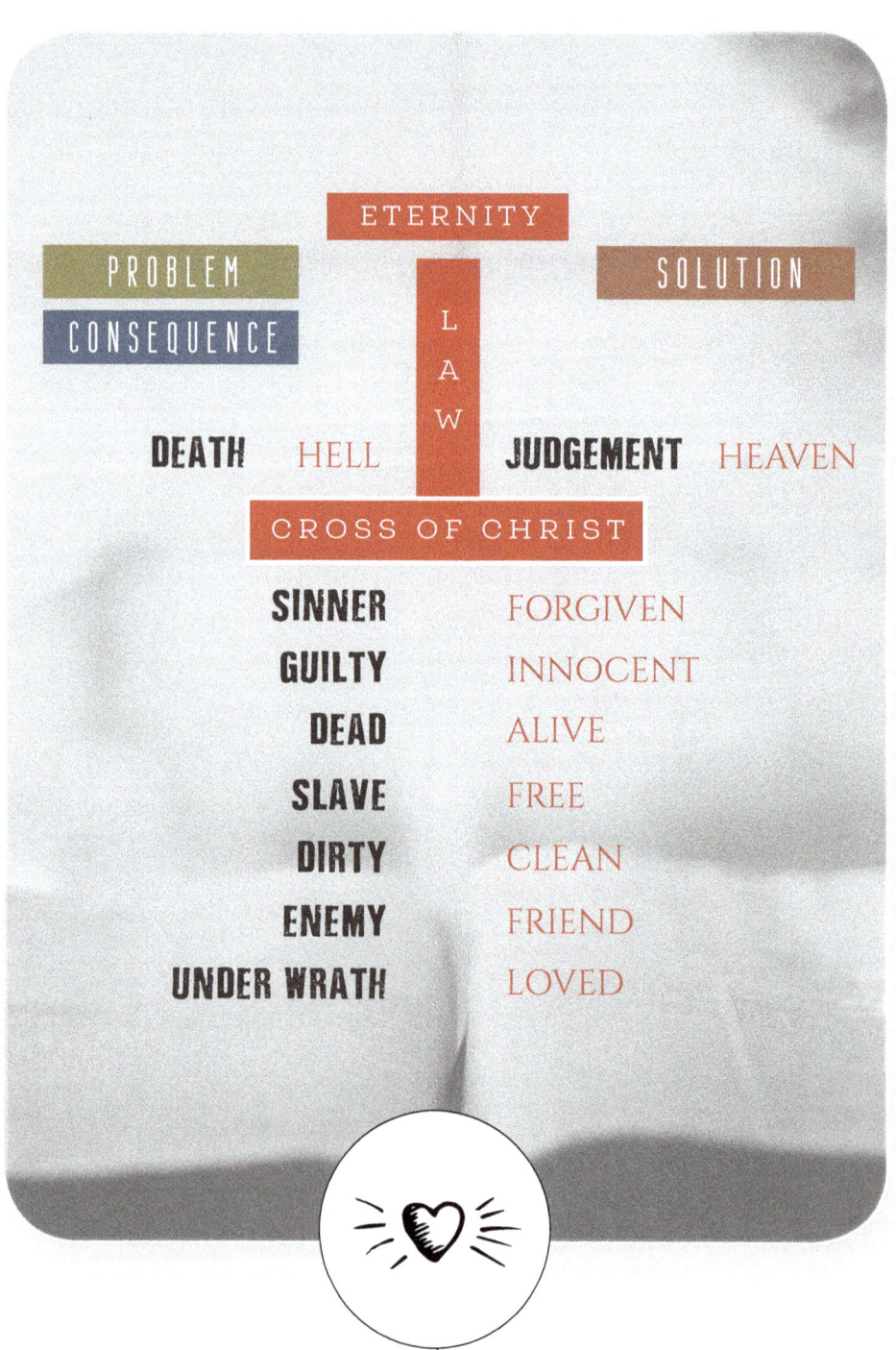

7. LOVED – JESUS IS YOUR PROPITIATION

> "In this is love, not that we have loved God but that he loved us and sent his Son to be the propitiation for our sins." (1 John 4:10)

Here are five things Jesus knows:

1. God's wrath is directed at sin.
2. You are full of sin.
3. The wrath of God abides on you.
4. On Judgement Day, you will be considered a child of wrath.
5. There is no hope for you to remove God's wrath by your own efforts — unless you find a substitute!

Watch Jesus in the Garden of Gethsemane the night before the cross. He knew He had to drink the cup of God's wrath for the sins that you committed. He asks for it to be removed, but then submits His will to the will of God, out of love for God and love for you.

> The cross is a redirection of God's wrath. God's wrath is aimed directly at you, and Jesus tells you to take refuge behind the cross. Then He takes your sin upon Himself and absorbs the wrath for you.

Jesus received the wrath you deserved so you could receive the love of God. This is good news!

Propitiation. Jesus became the target of God's wrath on the cross to satisfy God's justice so that His anger would be turned away from us.

TESTIMONY

When she was a teenager, Shirley disobeyed the curfew her mother had established for her and arrived home very late to face the consequences of her disobedience. When her older brother saw that Shirley was about to be punished, he stood between her and the imminent consequences and said, "Please don't punish her! Punish me instead!" Years later, when Shirley realized that she had also disobeyed a holy God and deserved His just punishment, she then understood that when Jesus died on the cross He stood between her and the righteous wrath of God and received the punishment that she deserved so that she could receive God's forgiveness. Shirley was grateful for what her brother did for her years earlier, but she is eternally grateful for what Jesus has done for her.

THE RESURRECTION

It is of great importance that within the message of the Cross, you explain the significance of the resurrection.

"And with great power the apostles were giving their testimony to the resurrection of the Lord Jesus, and great grace was upon them all."[87] In fact, nearly all of their messages included the resurrection.

Jesus urged His listeners to believe all that He taught. He told them to look at the miracles so they would be convinced He was from God and all He said was true. Finally, He said that He would prove that He came from God and spoke for Him. He said, "Destroy this temple." In other words, "Kill me."[88] He promised that His Father would raise Him up from the dead, thus proving the validity of His message.

> The resurrection is proof that all that Jesus taught is true.

But most significantly, the resurrection is proof that Jesus' death on the cross was sufficient to satisfy God's justice and settle the debt of our sin.

"He was given over because of our transgressions and was raised for the sake of our justification."[89] Jesus' resurrection is the proof that our debt was paid in full and God accepted His sacrifice on our behalf.

It is because of His resurrection that we can be born again. It is because Christ has been raised, our faith is not futile, and we are no longer in our sins.[90]

---

87 Acts 4:33
88 John 2:19
89 Romans 4:25
90 1 Corinthians 15:17

CHAPTER THREE: THE SOLUTION

REVIEW

The Power of the Cross

The preaching or sharing the message of the Cross is where much of the power of the gospel lies. Take note of the word "power" in these verses.

"For I am not ashamed of the gospel, for it is the **power** of God for salvation to everyone who believes."[91]

"For the word of the cross is folly to those who are perishing, but to us who are being saved it is the **power** of God."[92]

"But we preach Christ crucified, a stumbling block to Jews and folly to Gentiles, but to those who are called, both Jews and Greeks, Christ the **power** of God and the wisdom of God."[93]

Why Is the Message of the Cross So Powerful?

1. It pleases God. Jesus' work on the cross and the proclamation of that message is God's only way to save those who believe.[94]

2. Faith is released. Faith comes by hearing, which then allows people to believe and call upon the name of the Lord and be saved.[95]

3. Jesus is active. He is the one drawing the sinner to himself. "And I, when I am lifted up from the earth, will draw all people to myself."[96]

4. It leads to salvation. Jesus is the only way to the Father, and there is no other name under heaven given among men by which we must be saved.[97]

---

91 Romans 1:16
92 1 Corinthians 1:18
93 1 Corinthians 1:23-24
94 1 Corinthians 1:21
95 Romans 10:13
96 John 12:32
97 John 14:6; Acts 4:12

FINAL REMARKS

The solution God offered you through the Cross is amazing and mind-blowing. Yet, as good as the good news is, it can only be applied to your life through the fourth column. None of the good news is yours without the life-changing response of repentance and faith.

CHAPTER FOUR

Our Response

> *Back in 1982, I fell in love with 19-year-old Julie Gleason. I met her at Bible school, and my greatest desire was to get married and spend the rest of my life with her. I told her that I would renounce all three billion other women in the world if she would just say, "I do." I had no money or possessions, but I could offer her a lifetime of missions. I could offer her me.*
>
> *The day arrived when I was to ask for her hand in marriage. I was so nervous I broke out in an ugly case of acne and canker sores. That evening I got down on one knee and said, "Now for the time I have been waiting for – Julie Gleason, will you marry me?" End of story.*
>
> *Wait! So what was her response? You see, there is no wedding without an "I do." There is no marriage without Julie responding with a "yes."*
>
> *She said "yes."*

You need to say "yes" to Jesus. You need to respond to what He has done for you.

1. In the first column, you realized your problem when the Law proved you guilty of sin before God.
2. In the second column, the fear of God comes upon you as you realize that the consequence for your sin is eternal death.
3. In the third column, when you are without hope and without God in this world,[98] Jesus steps in and provides a solution to your problem via the cross, and gives you hope of eternal life.
4. The fourth column explains how to respond to Christ's offer of forgiveness.

The hope of eternal life is absolutely amazing; however, it is only a hope. It remains only an offer until the sinner responds to the message.

---

98 Ephesians 2:12

CHAPTER FOUR: OUR RESPONSE

Untold numbers of people are fully aware they are sinners and that God loves them "and died on the cross for their sins," and yet they do not have their names written in the book of life. On Judgement Day, they will hear the dreaded sentence, "Depart from me, I never knew you."[99]

Why? Because it is only information to them. They are religious, but they are not children of God. They worship Him with their lips, but their heart is far from Him.[100] They say Lord, Lord, but they do not do what He says.[101] There are many people in this situation. They haven't responded to the gospel in the way God commands.

---

[99] Matthew 7:23
[100] Matthew 15:8
[101] Luke 6:46

COLUMN FOUR
REPENTANCE AND FAITH

> "... but now he commands all people everywhere to repent, because he has fixed a day on which he will judge the world in righteousness by a man whom he has appointed..." (Acts 17:30-31)

1. CROSSING THE CROSS

There is a host of bad news on the left side of the cross, and there is an equal amount of good news on the right side of the cross. How do you "cross the cross?"

> You must respond favorably to what Jesus has done for you. To receive the good news of the gospel, you must repent and believe.

"The time is fulfilled, and the kingdom of God is at hand; repent and believe in the gospel."[102]

Beware of the wrong response.

We are NOT saved by going to church, being baptized, or teaching Sunday School. It is not enough to try to be a good person or work hard at following the Ten Commandments. Your name is not written in the book of life by repeating a prayer of faith or "accepting Jesus." That is not enough.

Many have put their faith in these things and, in the end, they will be cast away from God's presence.

The first thing God requires is repentance.

---

102 Mark 1:15

2. WHAT IS REPENTANCE?

You must repent and turn back to God if you want your sins to be blotted out.[103]

Repentance was a common word in the Greek language back in the time of Jesus. It did not begin as a religious word, however.

Let's say a man is headed toward Jerusalem, but along the way he gets lost. He approaches someone and inquires if he is on the road to Jerusalem. The man responds that he is not, and that, in fact, he is headed in the opposite direction. "Sir, you need to repent and head in that direction if you want to end up in Jerusalem."

Repentance is the awareness you are headed down the wide road to destruction. Therefore, you "change your mind" about staying on that road. You turn around and start walking on the narrow road that leads to life.

3. THE POWER OF THE HOLY SPIRIT

Up until this point, the power of the Holy Spirit has been extremely active through the first three columns.

1. The Holy Spirit convicts you of your sin.
2. The Holy Spirit convicts you of the judgement to come.
3. The Holy Spirit reveals Christ and His work on the cross for you.
4. Now God grants you repentance.

4. HOW DO I REPENT?

Repentance is a change of thinking, attitude, and action toward God and toward sin.

---

103 Acts 3:19

a) Change of Thinking (Your Mind)

When you repent, you agree with God and say, "God is right and I am wrong." This is what confession means. You see sin as God sees it, as sinful beyond measure.[104]

Imagine if someone offered you a piece of chocolate cake that was made with the best ingredients of flour, sugar, eggs, and butter. But then they told you it also had just a little bit of dog poop mixed in the batter. Would you eat it? Of course not, because dog poop is extremely disgusting! That is in a small measure how God sees lust, envy, pride, and immorality, as extremely disgusting![105] Once you see sin as God sees it, then you can say as the psalmist David after he was confronted about his sin, "Against you, you only, have I sinned and done what is evil in your sight."[106]

b) Change of Attitude (Your Emotions)

True repentance changes how you feel about your sin. You don't just feel bad because you have been caught in sin. But instead you feel deep sorrow for what you have done and for deeply offending a holy God. You have a sincere desire to change and get right with God.

c) Change of Action (Your Will)

Repentance involves making a decision to turn away from your sin and turn back to God.

Madrid has an excellent public transportation system of subways and commuter trains. But sometimes you can make the mistake of getting on a train going in the wrong direction. Once you realize you're going the wrong way, you've got to make the decision to get off the train, walk around to the other side, and get on the correct train that will take you to the right destination.

---

104 Romans 7:13
105 Aim for the Heart, Kevin Prevost, page 7-8
106 Psalm 51:4

You need to make the same decision with your life. When you realize that your sin is taking you the wrong way, you must decide to stop going in that direction, abandon your sin, turn around, and start following Jesus. Unless you make that decision, you will end up at the wrong destination.

Repentance Is a Command

"But God... now commands everyone everywhere to repent."[107] It is not just "accepting Christ." Christ needs to accept us, and that only happens through repentance.

5. WHAT IS FAITH?

Many are confused as to what it means to put your "faith, trust, or belief" in Jesus.

What saving Faith is NOT:

1. It is NOT intellectual assent only. The demons "believe," but they are not saved.[108] There are many religious people who only have an intellectual belief in God, and they are not saved.

2. It is NOT something without a foundation. The secular Merriam-Webster 2017 dictionary defines faith as: "a firm belief in something without evidence." Modern society understands "faith" as something lacking a foundation, or "blind faith." But true faith has a very firm foundation!

What saving Faith IS:

1. Surrender to Jesus. You put up the white flag, lay down your weapons, stop fighting against God and His will, and surrender to Him. In essence,

---

107 Acts 17:30
108 James 2:19

you say, "I give up," and recognize His authority over your life. You give Him the keys to your life and trust Him to drive you to His best destination.

2. Commitment. In a wedding ceremony, you renounce all former lovers and pledge your love to that one person for the rest of your life. When you commit to Jesus, you renounce all the sin you once loved and commit to love and obey Jesus for the rest of your life. You give Him your heart.

3. Dependence. Biblical faith is total dependence on God. The amazing story of Charles Blondin, a famous French tightrope walker, is a wonderful illustration of this.

> *Blondin's greatest fame came on September 14, 1860, when he became the first person to cross a tightrope stretched 1,100 feet across the mighty Niagara Falls. People from both Canada and America came from miles away to see this great feat.*
>
> *He walked across, 160 feet above the falls, several times... each time with a different daring feat – once in a sack, on stilts, on a bicycle, in the dark, and blindfolded. One time, he even carried a stove and cooked an omelet in the middle of the rope!*
>
> *A large crowd gathered and the buzz of excitement ran along both sides of the river. The crowd "Oohed and Ahhed!" as Blondin carefully walked across – one dangerous step after another – pushing a wheelbarrow holding a sack of potatoes.*
>
> *When he reached the other side, the crowd's applause was louder than the roar of the falls!*
>
> *Blondin suddenly stopped and addressed his audience: "Do you believe I can carry a person across in this wheelbarrow?"*
>
> *The crowd enthusiastically yelled, "Yes! You are the greatest tightrope walker in the world. We believe!"*
>
> *"Okay," said Blondin, "Who wants to get into the wheelbarrow?"*

As far as the Blondin story goes, no one did at the time!

This unique story is a real-life illustration of what faith actually is. The crowd watched these daring feats. They said they believed, but their actions proved they truly did not believe enough to trust him with their lives.

Similarly, it is one thing for us to say we believe in God. However, it's true faith when we put all of our trust in His Son, Jesus Christ.

Note: In August of 1859, Blondin's manager, Harry Colcord, did ride on Blondin's back across the Falls.[109]

REVIEW

Repentance and faith is your response to Jesus' call at the crossroads of your life.

- You begin your life following the wide road that leads to hell.
- You arrive at a crossroads, and Jesus invites you to follow Him.
- You have to make a decision to abandon your sin, turn around, and follow Jesus.
- There are times when you will trip and fall, but you don't stay there. You repent, Jesus lifts you up, and you continue to walk with Him; you don't return to the wide road of sin.

---

109 http://inspire21.com/stories/faithstories/CharlesBlondin

CHAPTER FOUR: OUR RESPONSE

FINAL REMARKS

Where is the power of repentance and faith?

When a sinner responds to Jesus with repentance and faith, there is…

1. A new birth.[110]

2. A new creation.[111]

3. Salvation from sin.[112]

4. Eternal life.[113]

5. Rejoicing in heaven. "There is joy before the angels of God over one sinner who repents."[114] Imagine that — with just one person repenting, all of heaven rejoices! I don't know of any single act that has the power to move heaven like repentance.

6. Crossing over from the bad news to the good news. Through repentance towards God and faith in Christ, there is the power to transport you from the left side of the cross to the right side, changing all of your bad news into good news!

---

110 John 3:3
111 2 Corinthians 5:17
112 Romans 1:16
113 1 John 5:11-12
114 Luke 15:10

TESTIMONY

As a young adult, Veronica moved to Madrid seeking God. One evening, she was crossing the main plaza, the Puerta del Sol, and was surprised to hear a woman on a red box joyfully singing about Jesus. Then a man began sharing a story about a judge and how one day we will stand before God and give account of our lives. Veronica was surprised to hear someone talking about her life and her sin, and she recognized that she was guilty before God. Then someone came alongside her and with grace and mercy explained how Jesus provided the solution to her sin problem through His death on the cross. Veronica's heart was prepared and right there in the plaza that night she repented of her sin and surrendered her life to Jesus. Her new friend began to disciple her, she became a Bible School student, and soon began to share her newfound faith with others.

REVIEW OF THE FOUR COLUMNS OF THE GOSPEL MESSAGE

The law of God shows us the bad news, that we are sinful, guilty of breaking God's commandments, spiritually dead, enslaved to sin, dirty, enemies of God, and deserving of God's wrath.

Eternity shows us the terrible eternal consequences of our sin.

The cross reveals how Jesus Christ saves us by paying for all of our bad news.

Now Jesus calls us to repent and surrender our lives to Him so we can get to the right side of the cross and obtain a right standing with God.

So, what about you?

"Examine yourselves, to see whether you are in the faith."[115]

On which side of the cross do you find yourself?

Have you surrendered your life to Jesus?

Have you seen your sin, your danger of hell?

Do you see Jesus hanging on that cross for you?

Have you renounced your sin and run to Jesus for forgiveness?

If it is so with you, then God offers you eternal life and you will be immediately:

---

[115] 2 Corinthians 13:5

1. Forgiven of all sin, the book erased.
2. Innocent. God's verdict of "not guilty" is yours.
3. Alive with the Holy Spirit dwelling in you.
4. Free from your chains of sin, Satan and the world.
5. Clean from the filth that excludes you from heaven.
6. A friend of God. All rebellion is removed. You have turned in your weapons.
7. Loved by God. You receive mercy instead of wrath.

This is the love of God.

> Why don't you take a moment to talk to Jesus right now? Repent of any known sin, and surrender your life to Him. Then thank Him for what He has done for you.

CONCLUSION

"I am not ashamed of the gospel, for it is the power of God for salvation to everyone who believes." (Romans 1:16)

The Importance of Sharing All Four Columns

Your assignment from Jesus is to proclaim the gospel message to every person.

As you proclaim the gospel, include all four columns in the message, for it is the power of God for salvation.

- If you remove the Law, what happens to the message? Without the Law to show us our sin, there is no problem. Without a problem, there are no consequences, and no need for a solution nor a response. Everything hinges on this first column. Until you understand your serious problem of sin, nothing else makes sense.

Yet many Christians are reluctant to talk about sin to avoid offending someone or making them feel bad. Like a caring doctor, you need to speak the truth in love, to explain the spiritual sickness so they will seek the life-saving treatment.

- If you remove eternity, what happens to the message? If there is no eternity, then there are no consequences. We may be guilty of committing sin, but if there is no judgement or afterlife, what does it matter?

Yet eternity is real! And, like Jesus, you need to warn others of the eternal consequences down the road in the hopes they will turn from the wide road that leads to destruction. Love compels us to warn others of the danger ahead.

- If you remove the Cross, what happens to the message? Without the Cross, there is no solution. We may be guilty and condemned to hell, but without the Cross, there is no hope.

As important as the Cross is, sadly, we frequently omit it from our evangelism, instead offering a Savior who will make our lives better, help our marriages, and make us rich or happy. Yet the Cross must be the center of the gospel message. Jesus came to die on the cross to set us free from our sin and give us eternal life.

- If you remove repentance and faith, what happens to the message? Without repentance and faith, there is no salvation. We may know we are guilty and headed for hell, and we may even know that Jesus died on the cross for our sins. But unless we repent and surrender our lives to Jesus, we cannot be saved. To repeat a "prayer of faith" or "accept Jesus" is not enough without true repentance and surrender to Him.

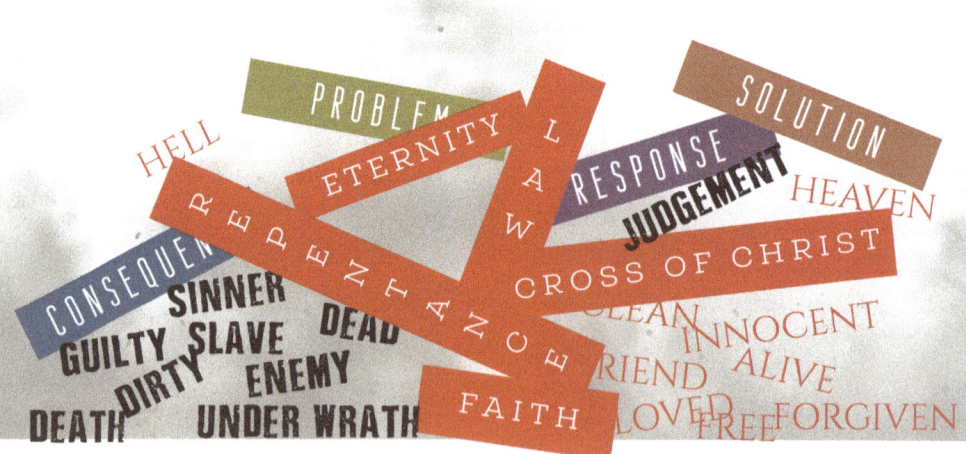

CONCLUSION

Each one of the four columns is essential to the message and demonstrates the power of God.

- The Holy Spirit convicts us of sin, of our horrible problem.
- The Holy Spirit convicts us of righteousness and of judgement, of the tragic consequences to our sin problem.
- The Holy Spirit reveals the wonderful work of Jesus on the cross and offers us a solution.

The Holy Spirit gives us new life when we repent and give our lives to Him.

The message of the Cross is powerful to transform lives!

> *When I returned to Spain from the revival services in America, my life had been transformed by the power of the gospel. I had an intense desire to fast and seek God. I became extremely sensitive to sin and didn't want to offend God in any way. My burden for souls increased significantly. My ministry became laser focused on preaching the message of the Cross.*
>
> *The ministry of ONTHEREDBOX[116], with its emphasis on cross-centered preaching, prayer, evangelism, and training evangelizers was born as a result of my encounter with the power of the gospel. It goes to show that the power of the gospel has the power to change the believer as well as the unbeliever.*

With whatever means you choose to proclaim the gospel, make a commitment to focus on the message of the Cross.

> "Knowing the fear of God, knowing that you too will stand before God and give an account, go out and persuade men." (2 Corinthians 5:11)

Jacob Bock

---

[116] ontheredbox.com

ABOUT THE AUTHOR

Jacob Bock first arrived in Spain in 1982 to evangelize in Alicante during the World Cup and there he received his call from God. Five years later, he came with his wife Julie to a church plant in Santiago de Compostela. From those early days to the present, whether involved in church planting, Festival of Light, teaching or itinerant ministry, Jacob's passion has been to reach the lost. His current ministry, On the Red Box, has branches in several countries in Europe and America. Seeing souls saved and training others to testify effectively has been the hallmark of a constant and faithful ministry in Spain and in many other parts of the world. Jacob Bock walks with God. This is evident because everything he does, bears fruit.

— Scott Smith

www.ingramcontent.com/pod-product-compliance
Lightning Source LLC
Chambersburg PA
CBHW042026100526
44587CB00029B/4315